THE B

———————— *to* ————————

THIRD AND FOURTH AGERS

Published by
The Bible Reading Fellowship
First Floor, Elsfield Hall
15–17 Elsfield Way, Oxford OX2 8FG
ISBN 1 84101 220 3

First published 2002
1 3 5 7 9 10 8 6 4 2 0

Acknowledgments

A catalogue record for this book is available from the British Library
Printed and bound in Great Britain by Omnia Books Limited, Glasgow

THE BIBLE SPEAKS

to

THIRD AND FOURTH AGERS

RICHARD L. MORGAN

'MAY YOU LIVE TO BE 120!'

An old Jewish blessing, said to date back to Moses' death

CONTENTS

INTRODUCTION

During 2000 my wife and I participated in 'The Year of the Bible' and read through the scriptures during the year. I was amazed at how often the Bible spoke to the issues of Third and Fourth Agers, either through role models or through a wisdom that addressed the needs of older persons. From that year-long reading of the Bible emerged this book of meditations. I decided on 120 readings, in tribute to Moses, of whom it was written, 'Moses was one hundred and twenty years old when he died; his sight was unimpaired and his vigour had not abated' (Deuteronomy 34:7).

As I reacquainted myself with biblical characters, what struck me was how relevant their approach to ageing was to us. Even across all the centuries, they still have the power to speak to us. Although we live in a different world from the one in which biblical writers lived, they still offer that eternal wisdom that speaks to every age.

In order to avoid patronizing and distasteful terms for older people, 'Third and Fourth Agers' seemed appropriate. Third Agers are active, vibrant and still involved in life. It is a time for new investment of energies, redirection and spiritual growth. The last third of life can be the richest part of our span of years. Fourth Agers, whose number will spiral in the coming years, may well have limited mobility, and suffer debilitating diseases. Ordinarily, Fourth Agers may be in sheltered housing or nursing homes, although an increasing number will stay in their own homes, provided with health care. This is a personal passage into dependence and frailty.

This book is written for all of us, those who are old, and those who have not yet had to face ageing, and for care-givers. Ageing does not just happen at one's 65th birthday. It happens to all of us, and happens as soon as we are born. A changing age profile confronts all the modern nations of the world, which are evolving from youthful to mature societies. The United Nations expects that by 2050 there will be nearly two billion people in the world 60 years or older, and by that same year, one of every five persons living will be 60 or older.

Carl G. Jung, one of the few psychologists who believed that the later years are a prime time for growth and fulfillment, once wrote, 'A human being would certainly not grow to be seventy or eighty years old if this longevity had no meaning for the species to which he belongs. The afternoon of human life must also have a significance of its own, and cannot be merely a pitiful appendage to life's morning'.[1] For Jung, the second half of life was a spiritual journey.

We have learned that we cannot grow towards wholeness or fight our way through the serious challenges of ageing alone. We have learned that finding strength in God will make our struggles easier. Surely, then, there is a crucial need to hear what the ageless word of God says to ageing humanity. Centuries ago, King Zedekiah asked the prophet Jeremiah, 'Is there any word from the Lord?' (Jeremiah 37:17). That remains the crucial question of old age: *Is* there any word from the Lord? We believe the Bible offers timeless wisdom for any age, and has special guidance for those in the later years.

GENESIS 11:27–32

HALFWAY HOUSES IN OLD AGE

Terah took his son Abram and his grandson Lot son of Haran, and his daughter-in-law Sarai, his son Abram's wife, and they went out together from Ur of the Chaldeans to go into the land of Canaan; but when they came to Haran, they settled there... and Terah died in Haran.

Abram and his father, Terah, had settled in a halfway house in Haran, a flourishing trade centre, several hundred miles to the north-west. Abram had been wrestling with a call from God to leave his country, but Haran had become a halfway house between his past and his future. Only when Terah died did Abram move on. Third and Fourth Agers often find themselves in halfway houses between a past that is over and a future yet to be.

It seems as if the later years are marked by periods of stability and periods of transition. There is no easy route from retirement to the grave. At first there is extended middle age, when ageing is acknowledged publicly and coincides with the end of a career. There is little decrease in energy or commitment or loss of control. But this stage ends when there are losses that require a significant change of lifestyle. These losses include the death or failing health of a spouse, or the decline of one's own physical well-being, and they demand that we forge a new identity and a new awareness of spiritual realities.

The final stage of ageing is marked by our own loss of physical health or mobility. No longer able to control our own life, we must now depend on others. Our days and nights are marked by taking pills, going to the doctor and struggling with endless infirmities.

As Abram maintained his close contact with God in that halfway house at Haran, so at any stage of ageing the secret to facing diminishments with courage is a vital faith in the God who carries us even in old age. A life lived in a one-to-one relationship with God will provide a foundation for strength right through to our very last breath.

God is with us through all the circling years, and each stage, each halfway house of ageing, can become a prime time for experiencing God's presence.

PRAYER

Ancient of Days, you never forsake us or fail us in our later years. In whatever halfway house we find ourselves, grant us your grace.

2

GOD CALLS US AT 75!

Now the Lord said to Abram, 'Go from your country and your kindred and your father's house to the land that I will show you. I will make of you a great nation, and I will bless you, and make your name great, so that you will be a blessing.' … So Abram went, as the Lord had told him.

Surely God did not call Abram when he was 75 years old! Biblical time must have been different from our time, and surely the call came in his middle years, the prime of life. It is then that we have the energy, initiative and intelligence to forge new directions and make a difference in the world. But believe it, Abram was 75 when God called him!

When his father, Terah, died, Abram could have returned to Ur of the Chaldeans and the highly developed culture and religion with which he was familiar. Or he could have settled in at Haran, a flourishing trade centre, and eked out his final years in well-deserved leisure.

Bu he was called to go to a strange, unknown land that God would show him—no map, no organized tour, not even a sure destination. The familiarity of Abram's call may mask the barriers to the trust required of him. Leave all that is familiar

13

in the disorienting times after a parent's death? Leave home for a land already heavily populated and claimed as home by others? Abram heard. Abram trusted. Abram obeyed God without a hint of doubt or disbelief... and the redemption of the world began to unfurl.

Third and Fourth Agers have three major temptations—to whine, recline or decline. Temptations exist to wallpaper the empty spaces with meaningless activities or dribble away the remaining years in idle nonsense. These years can be characterized by constant complaints.

But there is another way: *to shine*! That means waiting for God's call in the later years, and being willing to obey that call when we know it. As the prophet Habakkuk wrote, 'For there is still a vision for the appointed time... If it seems to tarry, wait for it; it will surely come, it will not delay' (Habakkuk 2:3).

A pensioner in the United Kingdom once told me, 'There are two kinds of older persons. The first sit by the porch and wait for the postman. The second stay active, and do the work of the Lord.' As surely as God called Abram at age 75, God calls us!

MEDITATION

Help me to be still and listen for your call, O God. Show me what I ought to be, not do.

3

Laughter of an old woman

Now Sarah was listening at the entrance to the tent, which was behind him. Abraham and Sarah were already old and well advanced in years, and Sarah was past the age of childbearing. So Sarah laughed to herself as she thought, 'After I am worn out and my master is old, will I now have this pleasure?' Then the Lord said to Abraham, 'Why did Sarah laugh? … Is anything too hard for the Lord?' … Sarah was afraid, so she lied and said, 'I did not laugh.' But he said, 'Yes, you did laugh.'

No wonder Sarah laughed. It was the honest response of an old woman who had enough life experience to know when something was downright funny. Imagine a 90-year-old woman having a child! She doubled over with laughter, as if someone was playing a cruel joke on her.

When the Lord chided Sarah for laughing at this promise, she was embarrassed, and denied her laughter. But she did laugh… and rightly so. She and Abraham knew that what was promised to them, a child in their old age, required a miracle. So they named the miracle child Isaac—'Laughter'—for as Sarah said, 'God has brought laughter for me; everyone who hears will laugh with me' (Genesis 21:6).

So we see that in a remarkable way the redemption of the world actually began with the laughter of two old people.

When we are older, and confronted with the inevitable pains and discomforts of ageing, God can make us laugh. Gold Meir said, 'Ageing is not a sin; but it isn't a joke either.' True—yet there can be humour in our later years.

Nurses and residents found a touch of humour in the depressing halls of a nursing home. A woman sauntered down the endless corridor, looking confused. A nurse asked if she could help, and the woman replied, 'I'm looking for some-one who has made a *faux pas*.' In a place where sadness and empty stares exist, she brought some laughter.

'A cheerful heart is a good medicine, but a downcast spirit dries up the bones' (Proverbs 17:22). How true! At a Bible study in a nursing home, one of the residents was reading the first Psalm. She stumbled over one verse, and read, 'On his law do I medicate day and night.' Everyone roared with laughter. That was the medication for the day. Let old men and old women laugh. It began with Sarah, and we can still hear her chuckles down through the centuries.

PRAYER

Lord, deliver me from being a sour, dour old person, but give me a sense of humour.

4

GENESIS 22:1–19

ANTICIPATED LOSS... MAJOR GAIN

After these things God tested Abraham... He said, 'Take your son, your only son Isaac, whom you love, and go to the land of Moriah, and offer him there as a burnt offering' ... Then Abraham reached out his hand and took the knife to kill his son. But the angel of the Lord called to him from heaven, and said... 'Do not lay your hand on the boy... for now I know that you fear God, since you have not withheld your son, your only son, from me.'

The story of Abraham's intended sacrifice of Isaac at Mount Moriah has to be one of the most powerful stories in the Bible. It was a test of Abraham's faith, not only because he dearly loved Isaac but because if he killed Isaac he would also kill the promise and wipe out the future of his people. We may be horrified by the demand of a capricious God, but we must see this story in the context of the times, when child sacrifice was the highest offering one could make.

The spotlight falls on old Abraham, who obeys this demand without questioning or arguing. Shaking like a leaf, the old man goes as far as raising the knife over Isaac's head, while the angels hold their breath. Then God speaks up at last, and says he has seen all he needed to see, and Abraham can sacrifice a ram instead.

The writer to the Hebrews comments on Abraham's faith, 'He considered the fact that God is able even to raise someone from the dead—and figuratively speaking, he did receive him back' (Hebrews 11:19). Abraham had vindicated God's faith in him. He was tested to give everything up, and his faith did not fail. His anticipated loss became a major gain.

Although older persons are not subjected to the same test as Abraham, we are nevertheless tested by losses that inevitably occur in old age. Our anticipated losses mean giving up mobility, youthful beauty and independence, and often sacrificing some of our dreams. But only those who take the knife in faith get Isaac!

It is only as we continue to trust God, and get beyond these losses, that we are blessed. God does provide for us, even as he provided a ram in the thicket for Abraham. Depth of soul, warm friendships, a caring church, become our rams in the thicket as we give up some of our strength and energy.

REFLECTION

What losses have I experienced in later life? What sacrifice from my earlier years have I been called on to make? Can I see how God does provide for me in these losses?

5

SILENT MOURNERS AT A
FATHER'S GRAVE

Abraham breathed his last and died in a good old age, an old man and full of years, and was gathered to his people. His sons Isaac and Ishmael buried him in the cave of Machpelah... There Abraham was buried, with his wife Sarah.

What a strange scene as Abraham was buried in the cave at Machpelah. Isaac and his half-brother, Ishmael, buried him in the same cave that Abraham had bought years before for the burial of Sarah. If either of them said anything while they buried their father, their words were not recorded. Perhaps the scene was played out in silence—the two old men, sons of the father, leaning on their shovels, out of breath, with their old father lying six feet deep beneath them. Did they cover their faces to hide their silent tears?

One wonders. Was Ishmael's expulsion into the desert forgotten? Was Sarah's cruelty to Hagar when the boys played together just a memory? Were Isaac and Ishmael reconciled as they said their farewells at their father's final resting-place? We do not know. The sand and stone at that grave keep their silence.

The death and burial of a parent always brings mingled feelings as the family gathers for the final rites. Sometimes stories are remembered and told as family members try to assuage their grief with memories of the departed loved one. At other times feelings of guilt prevail, the burden of unfulfilled promises and intentions. Or there may be stony silence, as unreconciled differences hover over the moment.

Freud said that the death of a parent is one of the most traumatic experiences of life: the loss leaves a void that nothing can fill. Some tend to believe that when an older parent dies, it is expected and requires no unusual grief. Simply not true!

Even when parents live to a good old age and die, like Abraham, 'old… and full of years', adult children mourn their loss. Somehow one chapter of life has ended and another begins. We feel bereft and sad. Perhaps that is how Isaac and Ishmael, fathers of nations, felt as they dropped their shovels and silently returned home—bereft and sad.

PRAYER

Gracious God, you have taught us to honour our fathers and mothers that our days may be long upon the land you have given us, so we honour them when they die, and cherish their memories.

GENESIS 26:17–22 (NKJV)

ISAAC: RECEIVING AND LEAVING THE PROMISE

And Isaac dug again the wells of water which they had dug in the days of Abraham his father, for the Philistines had stopped them up after the death of Abraham. He called them by the names which his father had called them.

It seems an insignificant, trivial thing, that Isaac dug again the wells of water which they had dug in the days of Abraham. The hated Philistines had stopped them up, but Isaac and his men reopened the wells and made the water flow again.

This redigging of the wells had more meaning than merely ensuring that water would flow. It was a symbol that the promise made to Abraham would not be stopped up, but would flow on to coming generations.

Isaac did nothing spectacular like his father, Abraham, or his son, Jacob. He was just a quiet man, who liked to sit in his tent, swat the flies, watch the sunset and wait for his favourite son, Esau, to bring him food. He played out his destiny with a quiet dignity.

But Isaac was a vital link between the generations in the

chain of the history of salvation. He received the promise, and he made sure he would leave it for the next generations. That is why the only tribute paid to him by the writer to the Hebrews in the roll call of the faithful is, 'By faith Isaac blessed Jacob and Esau concerning things to come' (Hebrews 11:20, NKJV).

Many older people feel their lives have made no difference, and they question whether any meaning can be found in their lives. Every life has meaning if we receive the faith and leave it for the next generation. Every life is a unique stone in the mosaic of human existence, especially as we reopen the wells of the past and become the channels through which the living water flows.

Like Isaac, we too have received the faith from our fathers and mothers. But our cosmetic culture and secularized world often stop up the wells of living water. Our task is to reopen those wells, rediscover the faith of our tradition and leave that faith for coming generations.

The psalmist prayed, 'The Lord of hosts is with us; the God of Jacob is our refuge' (Psalm 46:7, 11). Unless old Isaac, the quiet, unassuming patriarch, had reopened the wells of his father Abraham and handed down that ancient faith, Jacob might never have known that God.

REFLECTION

What is the faith we have received? How will we leave it for coming generations?

GENESIS 26:34–35; 27:46—28:5

BLESSINGS OF A DYSFUNCTIONAL FAMILY

When Esau was forty years old, he married Judith daughter of Beeri the Hittite, and Basemath daughter of Elon the Hittite; and they made life bitter for Isaac and Rebekah... Then Isaac called Jacob and blessed him, and charged him, 'You shall not marry one of the Canaanite women. Go... and take as wife... one of the daughters of Laban, your mother's brother.'

Ever since the twins Esau and Jacob staged a wrestling match in her womb, Rebekah never knew a moment of peace in the family circle. The boys were always at each other's throats, constantly trying to outwit the other. Jacob especially was good at winning the one-upmanship game, while Esau preferred the outdoors. As they sat at table in the family tent, Esau sat next to Isaac, and Jacob hung close to Rebekah.

When Esau married two Hittite woman, Rebekah's feud with her daughters-in-law served as an incentive to send Jacob off in search of a suitable spouse, thereby saving him from the murderous anger of his swindled brother, Esau. God turned the bitterness of that dysfunctional family into a blessing! For in Paddan-aram, Jacob found Rachel.

This biblical portrait of a dysfunctional family is all too familiar to us. We see it in our own families, as parents often operate control dramas, and children become master manipulators to get their own way. And what family has been spared parental favouritism or sibling rivalry? The old family story sounds all too contemporary.

An older woman was grieving the loss of her husband, and told why her loss was so great. 'I was always the unwanted child,' she said, 'and would stay in my room because my parents did not want me. My husband was the only person who ever accepted and affirmed me.'

God does not turn his back on dysfunctional families. God works in strange ways to turn rejection and bitterness into redemption and blessing. The bitterness of Esau's marriages and the rejection of the Hittite women led to Jacob's journey and a joyous marriage.

This story calls us to be more tolerant of family members whose blemishes seem to spoil the family portrait, as well as to look for the amazing ways our rejection can become God's blessing.

REFLECTION

Picture your birth family in your mind. What imperfections or bitterness spoil the portrait? Can you now discern how God turned these blemishes into blessings?

GENESIS 31:43–50

THE REAL MEANING OF THE MIZPAH BENEDICTION

*Laban said, 'This heap is a witness between you and me today.'
Therefore he called it Galeed, and the pillar Mizpah, for he said,
'The Lord watch between you and me, when we are absent one
from the other.'*

For many years, these words became the pious Mizpah benediction, spoken at the end of religious meetings. As we parted we prayed that God would watch over us and protect us. These nice words have also been used at weddings or when persons are absent from each other, as a prayer for God's protection and blessing.

But this was not the original meaning of the Mizpah benediction. Two old tricksters had come to the parting of the ways. Laban, Jacob's uncle, had tricked him many times. Laban's daughter Rachel was the love of Jacob's life, and Laban took advantage of that budding romance to turn it to his own profit. He palmed off the weak-eyed Leah for seven years of labour from Jacob. And Jacob had done his share of tricks, too, using cleverness to acquire wealth and flocks from Uncle Laban.

As they parted, the Mizpah benediction really meant, 'May God keep his eye on you and me when we cannot keep our eyes on each other, for the Lord knows what we will do next.' They were not words of confidence, but of suspicion; not sweet sentiment, but mutual distrust.

Older persons must constantly be vigilant about abuse either by financial exploitation or passive neglect. Regrettably, much of that abuse comes from the families, the care-givers. Because the abuse is usually done by someone close, most abused persons suffer in silence. They would rather risk the abuse than to live alone or be sent to a nursing home.

Jesus taught the disciples that we must be 'wise as serpents and innocent as doves' (Matthew 10:16). The words exchanged between Jacob and Laban showed a shrewd wisdom based on experience. Too many older people allow themselves to be taken in by those who would take advantage of them or prey on their vulnerability.

Like the original content of the Mizpah benediction, we need the wisdom of Jacob and Laban that God will watch over our lives and save us from those who would trick us, even our own families!

PRAYER

Lord, help me as an older person to stay in control of my life, and not let others take advantage of me.

GENESIS 32:22–33 (NIV)

NOT GENTLE INTO THE GOOD NIGHT

So Jacob was left alone, and a man wrestled with him until daybreak… Then the man said, 'Let me go, for it is daybreak.' But Jacob replied, 'I will not let you go unless you bless me.' The man asked him, 'What is your name?' 'Jacob,' he answered. Then the man said, 'Your name shall no longer be Jacob, but Israel, because you have struggled with God and with men and have overcome.'

Jacob was 60 years old when he returned to Canaan, his original home. He was now a successful wheeler-dealer who had often outwitted his Uncle Laban. No longer the little mamma's boy who hid behind her skirts, he was now a man of power and wealth. His own manipulative tricks and cleverness made him feel he was the master of his fate, a self-made man.

Yet as he approached the ford of the River Jabbok, his heart trembled, for Esau was on his way with 400 armed men, bent on revenge. Jacob sent his entourage to safety behind him, and sat alone in the darkness, struggling with his past. Little did he know that he would not go gently into the good night, but through painful struggle that night he would be changed.

All night long, Jacob wrestled with God, and as the day broke, Jacob refused to surrender his hold on this strange, midnight assailant. So finally he was blessed with a new beginning as one day ended and another began.

Dr G. Campbell Morgan wrote, 'God crippled him to crown him, revealed his weakness to teach him the secret of strength, defeated him that he might find the victory. How often disabilities are the signs of royalty, and so of ability.'[2] Jacob became the wounded healer. Halted in his tracks by his wounded side, he surrendered his old self-reliance, and became the new Israel.

As older persons, we struggle with the inevitable issues of ageing. Chronic disabilities and crippling losses come even to those in good health. That fateful hour comes when we must give up our independence and rely on others… and God. Like Jacob, the wounds of old age can become the very place where new life begins and the moment when we trust God. And those same wounds can become our vulnerability which we can share with others for their blessing.

REFLECTION

Take a second look at some of the issues with which you wrestle as an older person. Can they become moments of grace?

10

UNEXPECTED RECONCILIATION

Now Jacob looked up and saw Esau coming, and four hundred men with him… But Esau ran to meet him, and embraced him, and fell on his neck and kissed him, and they wept… Jacob said, '…for truly to see your face is like seeing the face of God—since you have received me with such favour.'

The dreaded moment had come when Jacob had to meet Esau, the twin brother whom he had tricked out of the birthright and the blessing. Jacob went unarmed, frightened, and yet believing God would see him through. He bowed respectfully before Esau, offering him gifts to curry his favour. What a different man this Jacob is from the arrogant youth who denied the famished Esau a bowl of soup! Jacob expected violent retribution from this powerful brother. He had no illusions of a sentimental reunion.

Instead Esau embraces him, and they both weep. Two brothers hold each other in their arms as old hatreds dissolve and heaven approves. Jacob, overcome with emotion, says, 'Truly to see your face is like seeing the face of God.' Esau's unconditional acceptance was a prototype of God's unconditonal love.

The story is a reversal of the parable Jesus told of two brothers (Luke 15:11–32). Unlike the older brother who sulked and pouted and would not join the party or accept his brother, Esau makes the party. He is more like the father in Jesus' story who loves the prodigal without reservation. Jacob, the prodigal, returns home, not to the expected vengeance of an angry victim but to the unexpected love of a brother.

We do not know what was happening to Esau in those years since Jacob had betrayed him. His genuine spirit indicates that somehow God had helped Esau overcome his anger and forgive his brother.

As life extends into old age, there is a strong need to make peace with those who have wronged us. We do not want to continue to carry with us unresolved anger or broken relationships. Time is stretchable; we can reframe and reshape it. We can reach back into the past and repair broken relationships. We can reach out to those who have hurt us and forgive them.

This story ends on a happy note, with reconciliation between brothers. It doesn't always happen. But even when reconciliation doesn't take place, letting go of bitterness that poisons our spirits brings wholeness.

REFLECTION

Recall any person who has hurt you in your life and forgive them… and bless them.

GENESIS 35:16–20 (NJB)

JACOB'S GREATEST LOSS

They left Bethel, and while they were still some distance from Ephrath, Rachel went into labour, and her pains were severe. When her labour was at its hardest, the midwife said to her, 'Do not worry, this is going to be another boy.' At the moment when she breathed her last, for she was dying, she named him Ben-Oni. His father, however, named him Benjamin. So Rachel died and was buried on the road to Ephrath, now Bethlehem.

Rachel was Jacob's greatest love. He had worked fourteen years to become her husband, but they seemed like a few days, so great was his love for her. Rachel was pregnant, and on the road to Ephrath she went into labour and died in childbirth.

In her dying anguish she named the son Ben-Oni, 'son of my sorrow'. Jacob, refusing to let his son bear such an unlucky name throughout life, named him Benjamin, 'son of the right hand', or 'child of good luck'.

No doubt Jacob was grief-stricken when Rachel died. Like a deer that stands frozen in the headlights of a car, it seemed as if Jacob's life had come to a screeching halt. The death of a spouse calls us to question all the certainties of life and death. The fragmenting world holds little joy. Friends rally at the time of death, then forget, and the loneliness can become unbearable.

One wonders what Jacob felt as he buried Rachel outside the city of Bethlehem. His days would be coloured with grey, his nights long and endless. But the text says, 'Israel journeyed on, and pitched his tent beyond the tower of Eder' (Genesis 35:21). His grief may have made him wish to die and be buried near Rachel, but he journeyed on. He had a family to care for, a new child, and the family of Israel. So he said his goodbyes at the grave, as life moved slowly on.

Rachel was buried outside Bethlehem. Later in holy history, another child is born in Bethlehem. This time both mother and child live, but other children die in Bethlehem, as 'a voice was heard... Rachel weeping for her children' (Matthew 2:18). It is also through the child born in Bethlehem, who tasted death for every person, that the sting of death is removed. Letting go, moving on: grief over the loss of a spouse demands no less.

REFLECTION
Visualize a circle of light and, if your spouse has died, imagine they stand in the centre of that light. What would you say to them now?

GENESIS 35:27–29 (NJB)

THE MELLOWING OF JACOB

Jacob came home to his father Isaac at Mamre... where Abraham and Isaac had stayed. Isaac was one hundred and eighty years old when he breathed his last. He died and was gathered to his people, an old man who had enjoyed his full span of life. His sons Esau and Jacob buried him.

They stood in silence at their father's grave, those twin brothers, now themselves old men. Estranged for years, separated by miles, now they were true brothers, saying goodbyes to their aged father.

What a change had taken place in both of their lives! Esau's hot temper and hostility against his brother had dissolved. And what a change in Jacob! The rascal who had cheated Esau out of what was coming to him, and treated his old, blind father as a fool, had mellowed.

Now Jacob stood at the grave and buried that past as the dirt covered Isaac's body. His days of productivity and achievement had ended. He was now a widower, still grieving the loss of Rachel—a patriarch who lived with his other wives and many sons. He still made mistakes, but they were the errors of the heart, the failings of a man who loved deeply.

Jacob had mellowed. Now he was Israel, responsible father and grandfather of the chosen people.

Some believe that older people cannot change, but remain the same person they've always been. We do bring to old age the person we have been all our lives. That means continuity of our identity—that we are who we have been. However, we can mellow and age gracefully.

Retirement is not a time to retreat, regress or withdraw from life. It is a time to grow in character, to become resilient in adversity. Like Jacob, we will face many obstacles and adversities. Life will be hard, even for those who seem to avoid difficulties.

We have the choice, to be bitter or better, grumpy or gracious. Much will be taken from us—strength, physical beauty, loved ones and friends. But we can display the qualities of soul that come with character, as Peter wrote, 'The inner self with the lasting beauty of a gentle and quiet spirit, which is very precious in God's sight' (1 Peter 3:4).

REFLECTION
Pray the prayer of Teresa of Avila: 'From silly devotions and from sour-faced saints, good Lord, deliver us.' Amen.

WHEN GOD CHANGES HIS PLANS

When Israel set out on his journey with all that he had and came to Beer-sheba, he offered sacrifices to the God of his father Isaac. God spoke to Israel in visions of the night, and said, 'Jacob, Jacob.' And he said, 'Here I am.' Then he said, 'I am God… do not be afraid to go down to Egypt, for I will make of you a great nation there. I myself will go down with you to Egypt, and I will also bring you up again; and Joseph's own hand shall close your eyes.'

God spoke these words to Jacob, very near the close of the fascinating story of his life. In calling him twice by his old name, Jacob, God reminded him of his past. At this time Jacob was about one hundred and thirty years old, and after a life of perils, toils and snares he had finally found peace in the land that God had given to Abraham and Isaac. Surely now he could rest in his tents and enjoy the final days.

However, God changed Jacob's plans. God called him to leave his quietness and rest and to go down to Egypt, the very land to which his grandfather Abraham had warned him not to go. Egypt was unknown—a place of foreboding and trouble. Why was God abandoning his plan and asking him to retrace his grandfather's journey into an unknown land? But Jacob was confident that God would go with him, and one day bring him back to his home.

Older persons continually find that life brings its 'wake-up calls', demanding change and forging a new life identity. At times it means relocation from one's home to sheltered housing or a nursing home. At other times it is the death of a spouse, or deterioration of one's own or a spouse's physical well-being.

We prefer that life should remain as it was, and we are fearful of these major changes that force us to find a new identity. Our 'Egypt' may well be where we do not want to go, but we find comfort that God goes with us, going ahead to prepare the way. The words of the hymn teach us this faith:

God of the coming years, through paths unknown
We follow Thee;
When we are strong, Lord, leave us not alone;
Our refuge be.
Be Thou for us in life our daily bread,
Our heart's true home when all our years have sped.
HUGH THOMPSON KERR (1871–1950)

PRAYER
Let us be ready, O God, for whatever lies ahead; and when the inevitable changes of later life make their demands on us, give us the assurance that you will be our strength and shield.

GENESIS 49:1–33

JACOB SAYS GOODBYE

Then Jacob called his sons, and said: 'Gather around, that I may tell you what will happen to you in days to come. Assemble and hear, O sons of Jacob; listen to Israel your father…' Then he charged them, saying to them, 'I am about to be gathered to my people. Bury me with my ancestors…' When Jacob ended his charge to his sons, he drew up his feet into the bed, breathed his last, and was gathered to his people.

Jacob was fully aware that his death was imminent. Although he lived in Egypt, his life had ended with unbelievable joy. He had been reunited with his favourite son, Joseph, whom he had given up as dead. The time had come to say goodbye, so he gathered his twelve sons around his deathbed. He looked into the faces of sons he could hardly see, gave each of them a blessing, and charged them to bury him in the cave in the field of Machpelah. This meant a sad funeral procession of three hundred miles, much of it through the rocky barrens of the wilderness of Shur. So, as if he was rehearsing a later homecoming, Jacob made his funeral plans and died a happy man.

Although goodbyes are always difficult, the final goodbyes

are the hardest. We say our goodbyes in this life, but they are softened by the assurance that we will meet again; but when death closes in on a loved one, this is so hard, for when they breathe their last, it is over.

Jacob knew that saying goodbye was important for himself and his family. It meant closure for the dying person to say goodbye, but it was meaningful for family and friends to say their goodbyes, too.

Henri Nouwen has written, 'Real grief is not healed by time. It is false to think that the passing of time will slowly make us forget her and take away our pain... If time does anything, it deepens our grief.'[3]

We can only imagine what the sons of Jacob said to their dying father. Did they ask forgiveness for their cruelty to Joseph? Did they ask Jacob to intercede with Joseph, for fear that he would still bear a grudge against them and pay them back? And how did Joseph say goodbye to his father? We recall when Joseph first saw his father after so many years, Joseph was so overwhelmed with emotion that he 'wept on his neck a good while' (Genesis 46:29). But now it was time to say goodbye for ever. Saying goodbyes is always hard, but it is vital to healing the loss.

REFLECTION

Visualize that you are dying, and your family gathers around your bed. How would you say goodbye?

WHY MOVE JOSEPH'S BONES?

Then Joseph said to his brothers, 'I am about to die; but God will surely come to you, and bring you up out of this land to the land that he swore to Abraham, to Isaac, and to Jacob.' So Joseph made the Israelites swear, saying, 'When God comes to you, you shall carry up my bones from here.' And Joseph died, being one hundred and ten years old; he was embalmed and placed in a coffin in Egypt.

It is interesting to observe how children tend to become like their parents, especially in later life. Joseph mirrored his father Jacob's dying wish. Neither of them wanted to be buried in Egypt. Unlike Jacob, Joseph did not insist that his bones be moved immediately after his death. Instead, in the belief God would bring Israel back to Canaan, he wanted his descendants to take his bones with them.

In a way, these were strange funeral plans, since Joseph had not lived in Canaan since he was a boy. He had been back once, to bury Jacob. He must have had some bitter memories of how his brothers sold him into slavery. But these memories had been transformed by his experience in Egypt. Furthermore, his coffin would have much greater pomp and glory in Egypt. In Egypt, they buried their significant people with majestic rites, and it was in Egypt that Joseph had gained his power and honour. Joseph was determined that his bones would bear witness to God's exodus promise. Four hundred years later, when the children of Israel fled Egypt on that dark Passover night, we read that 'Moses took with him the bones of Joseph' (Exodus 13:19), and according to tradition, Joseph's bones were buried in Shechem.

Christians cannot help but recall that dark Saturday when the bones of Jesus were placed in a stone-sealed tomb that served as a coffin. Between 3pm on Good Friday and some time after Holy Saturday's midnight, Jesus' body lay in a far more desolate Egypt, the tomb of Joseph of Arimathea. All of creation tottered between despair and hope.

Just as God did not allow Joseph's bones to be forgotten in an Egyptian coffin, so God did not allow Jesus to be held by death. As God brought Israel out of Egypt, so God raised Jesus from the grave, and ended once for all the nightmare of sin.

REFLECTION

Remember the committal services of loved ones. Where did they take place? What were your thoughts at that time? What are they now?

16

Exodus 3:1–12

Moses: 're-fired' at 80!

There the angel of the Lord appeared to him in a flame of fire out of a bush; he looked, and the bush was blazing, yet it was not consumed. Then Moses said, 'I must turn aside and look at this great sight…' God called to him out of the bush, 'Moses, Moses!' And he said, 'Here I am.'

Moses was eighty years old when God called him to his destiny. Strengthened by forty years in the wilderness, tempered by the rigours of the desert, Moses was ready to respond to the needs of his people. But this late life-call came unexpectedly. He had been a simple shepherd, tending sheep in the land of Midian. He had no idea that God would call him to shepherd Israel. Nor did he know that this call would mean forty years of putting up with a grumbling congregation who would resist his leadership and constantly rebel against his judgments.

How appropriate that the call came through fire, for God was re-firing this man of faith and making him a pillar of fire for Israel. Moses was amazed that the bush burned, yet it was not consumed. Despite his advanced age, the fire still burned in Moses' heart. He could not forget the harsh bondage of his people, nor how the flame of hope burned dimly in their hearts.

We need to strike the word 'retirement' from our vocabulary, and replace it with the word 're-firement'. Retirement connotes retreat, regression, withdrawal. It suggests that when you pack in your briefcase there is little left in life except killing the time you have saved. Read the scriptures, and there is little mention of God's people retiring! Rather, God's call comes at any age, and the call that comes in later life may be the most important of all.

Pensioners are not to be shelved or shunted to the sidelines. At times, older people are their own worst enemies, when they play the helpless recipients and give the impression that they always want things done for them. Moses became a role model of late-life leadership. He lit a fire for all of Israel because he was re-fired. As long as God's call burns in our hearts, it cannot be extinguished by those who would discard us, make us passive recipients, or discount us as persons.

PRAYER

God of Abraham, Isaac, Jacob and Moses; God of fire; don't let anyone quench my fire. Re-fire me in my older age.

17

EXODUS 14:10–14, 21–23

WHEN OLDER PEOPLE FEEL TRAPPED

As Pharaoh drew near, the Israelites looked back, and there were the Egyptians advancing on them. In great fear the Israelites cried out to the Lord… Then Moses stretched out his hand over the sea. The Lord drove the sea back by a strong east wind all night, and turned the sea into a dry land… The Israelites went into the sea on dry ground.

It seemed like an impossible situation. The Israelites were trapped between the chariots of the onrushing Egyptian border police and the sea. Disaster seemed imminent. There was no way out; only certain death awaited them.

The book of Exodus gives us two accounts of the crossing of the sea, combined into one story. In one account, a strong east wind blew the waters back all night, and left a sandbar for the Israelites to scamper to safety (14:21).

In the later account, the water piled up like walls on both sides of the pathway (14:22)—the Cecil B. DeMille account! No one knows for certain what did happen at the Yam Suph (Sea of Reeds). However it happened, Yahweh delivered Israel from disaster and it left an indelible impression on them for evermore.

A little boy was asked by his church school teacher to draw a picture of the crossing of the sea. He coloured the whole page a vivid red. When the teacher asked, 'Where are the Israelites?' he replied, 'Gone over to the other side.'

'Well, then, where are the Egyptians?'

'They have all drowned,' he replied.

Older people often feel they are trapped, with no way back or way out. Sometimes they are facing relocation from home. On the one hand, they don't want to give up their homes, but on the other hand, they want to please family members and not be a burden. At other times, older people feel trapped in the strange limbo between being independent and too dependent on others. Like the Israelites, they feel hopelessly trapped.

Moses urged the Israelites, 'Do not be afraid, stand firm, and see the deliverance that the Lord will accomplish for you today' (Exodus 14:13). Like the Israelites, older people need to plunge ahead, take the risks that change demands, and forge a new future.

PRAYER

Loving God, when life hems us in and we feel trapped, give us faith to see how you will provide a way through.

18

EXODUS 17:8–16

DEPENDING ON OCTOGENARIAN PRAYERS

But Moses' hands grew weary; so they took a stone and put it under him, and he sat on it. Aaron and Hur held up his hands, one on one side, and the other on the other side; so his hands were steady until the sun set.

The Israelites were locked in a major battle with the Amalekites at Rephidim. Moses stood on the mountain with his staff, the symbol of his spiritual power, in his hand. As long as Moses held up his arms in prayer, the battle went in favour of Israel. But when from sheer weariness his arms began to fall, the tide turned against Israel.

Aaron and Hur, two octogenarians, held up Moses' arms, and once again Israel prevailed. It proved to be those intercessory hands of prayer on the mountain and not just the might of arms in the valley that controlled the tide of battle.

Old as they were, these octogenarians supported Moses with their prayers and brought victory to God's people. Their ministry of intercession and support not only upheld Moses, but also strengthened the cause of Joshua and his men struggling on the battlefront.

Older people need to realize the power of prayer. I remember one 96-year-old lady in a nursing home who hadn't been able to attend her church for years. Her arthritic hands made it difficult for her to hold a Bible, and her fading eyesight wouldn't allow her to read the words anyhow.

But she prayed for every member of the church by name every day. She visualized their faces and prayed for them in her room. She prayed for her pastors, too, and asked God to sustain them when their hearts grew weary in the work. She prayed for her church. One has to believe that her prayers kept the windows of that church open to another world.

God's oldest friends can be prayer warriors, even when they are forced to be on the sidelines, away from the main action. Romano Guardini wrote, 'For a Christian in old age only one thing can be at the core of life—prayer.' As Richard Bach has said, 'Here is the test to find whether your mission on earth is finished—if you're alive, it isn't'.[4]

REFLECTION

Aaron's and Hur's prayers upheld and supported Moses. Think of a person who needs your prayer and visualize them, and offer prayers on their behalf.

19

EXODUS 18:13–27 (NJB)

LEARNING TO RELY ON ELDERS

Moses' father-in-law then said to him, 'What you are doing is not right. You will only tire yourself out, and the people with you too, for the work is too heavy for you. You cannot do it all yourself... Choose capable and God-fearing men... and put them in charge... They will refer all important matters to you, but all minor matters they will decide themselves, so making things easier for you by sharing the burden with you.'

Moses was overwhelmed by the demands of the people. Like a bedouin chief, Moses acted as judge in the people's disputes. People stood outside his tent from morning to evening, asking for his advice and judgment. The excessive demands were more than Moses could handle. So his father-in-law, Jethro, an older man, advised Moses to delegate minor matters to elders, who would make things easier for him by sharing the burden.

This story speaks to older people for three reasons:

- Moses took the advice of an older man, his father-in-law. Unlike King Rehoboam, who discounted the advice of the older men, and followed his younger friends, Moses wisely listened to Jethro. When Rehoboam discounted the advice and help of the elders, he plunged the nation into a civil war (1 Kings 12).

- The men to whom these matters were delegated were older 'God-fearing men', whose wisdom was well sanctioned by the community, and who had the time to handle these situations.
- The elders who volunteered to help Moses with these tasks were willing to give their time and become permanent judges, handling minor matters, but referring hard cases to Moses.

This story is a model for the contemporary church. Clergy are hard pressed to handle all the demands of a congregation. Some want to be 'lone rangers', trying to do everything. This can lead to early burn-out and unnecessary stress.

Elders who are willing to play cameo roles, or handle minor matters, can be of inestimable value in the work of the church. They are available, and their wisdom does not need to be ignored. By attending to some of the minor matters in the life of the congregation, they can free the pastor for the work of ministry.

PRAYER

Lord, help me to realize my value as an older person, and to offer my wisdom and experience to help your church.

20

EXODUS 32:1–6, 15–24 (NJB)

AARON: OLD MAN'S ALIBI

And there, as he approached the camp, [Moses] saw the calf and the groups dancing. Moses blazed with anger... Moses then said to Aaron, 'What have these people done to you for you to have brought so great a sin on them?' Aaron replied, '...They said to me, "Make us a god to go at our head; for that Moses, the man who brought us here from Egypt—we do not know what has become of him." I then said to them, "Anyone with gold, strip it off!" They gave it to me. I threw it into the fire, and out came this calf!'

Moses came down from the mountain, with the law of God on his heart and the commandments written in stone. For forty days and nights he had been in the presence of God.

When Moses had failed to descend from the mountain, a panic swept through the people. They assumed Moses had died on Mount Sinai. Without Moses, they felt insecure and utterly abandoned. They wanted a god they could see and touch, so they persuaded Aaron to make a golden calf which would stand between them and their uncertainty.

Moses confronted Aaron, who made up alibis to escape the heat. Refusing to accept responsibility as the leader, he first blamed the people, and then offered the flimsy excuse that the people gave him their gold, and when he tossed it into the fire—hey presto!—out came a golden calf! As a leader, he could have prevented the crafting that went into making his golden calf. But he went along with the wishes of the crowd.

Aaron's alibi—blame the people, blame circumstances. We call this 'scapegoating', refusing to accept responsibility for our actions and blaming others for our sins. It began in the Garden of Eden when Adam blamed Eve, and Eve blamed the serpent, and it has happened ever since that time.

Older people can be good at scapegoating. Sometimes we blame our adult children, finding fault with them when life is hard. Or we can blame our care-givers, and constantly find fault with them. It takes courage to take responsibility for our actions, to say in the words of Cassius, 'The fault, dear Brutus, is not in our stars, but in ourselves' (Shakespeare, *Julius Caesar*, Act I Scene 2). Projecting our problems on to others thwarts our growth. Accepting responsibility for our lives is the way to growth, even in old age.

PRAYER

Help us, O God, to be responsible for our decisions, and not to blame others when things don't go as we wished.

21

NUMBERS 8:23-26

WHEN RETIREMENT IS MENTIONED IN THE BIBLE

The Lord spoke to Moses, saying: This applies to the Levites: from twenty-five years old and upward they shall begin to do duty in the service of the tent of meeting; and from the age of fifty years they shall retire from the duty of the service and serve no more. They may assist their brothers in the tent of meeting in carrying out their duties, but they shall perform no service.

It is often said that 'retirement' is not mentioned in the Bible—but it is mentioned! In a sermon entitled 'Fifty Years— and After', preached at Westminster Chapel, London, in 1913, G. Campbell Morgan discussed the retirement of the Levites.

In their working years, the Levites took up all the work of the office, carrying their portion of the sacred tent and furniture from place to place, and doing all the hardest work of the tabernacle system of worship. At fifty, the Levites were released from routine work, and were set free from the more exacting duties that made demands upon their physical strength.

Although retired, their service continued. They became volunteers in the holy place, teaching the law and being available for counsel and guidance. Morgan said this about retirement:

What we ask of life is that we may be set free from certain forms of service, not for idleness, but that we may do less for the doing of more; in order that we may employ the great gains the years have brought to us in the interest of our fellow man; in order that with increasing faith we may encourage dawning faith.[5]

We live in a society that worships retirement. How odd that we should spend all our lives doing something so that we don't have to do it any more. Retirement may be a time to slow down, and not get up and go to work every day. But that doesn't mean we stop living and withdraw completely from the mainstream of life.

As the Levites retired *from* one form of service, *to* another kind of service, so retirement is but another transition in the journey of life. All the experience and skills we have accumulated over a lifetime need to be harvested so that we can offer ourselves to the service of God.

PRAYER

Ancient of Days, we may be retired from the world of work, but we never retire from the service of God. Show us how we can be used for your service.

22

USED, NOT PATRONIZED

Moses said to Hobab son of Reuel the Midianite, Moses' father-in-law, 'We are setting out for the place of which the Lord said, "I will give it to you"; come with us, and we will treat you well…' But he said to him, 'I will not go, but I will go back to my own land and to my kindred.' He said, 'Do not leave us, for you know where we should camp in the wilderness, and you will serve as eyes for us.'

The Israelites were on the eve of their departure from Sinai to go into the promised land. Moses tried to persuade his father-in-law, Hobab (also known as Jethro), to go with them. First Moses promised him that he would be treated well, but Hobab declined.

Moses then challenged him and asked for his help. Hobab's knowledge of the wilderness would be of great service. His old eyes would be their map through this unknown land. The second appeal was accepted, for Hobab wanted a challenge, not a cushion.

The *Ford Times* told about a certain farmer who bought an old Ford in 1909, and kept it in the parlour of his home. The hired girl polished it once a week, and the owners admired it but never took it out on the road. They were afraid that the old Ford would disintegrate and fall apart. It sat in the parlour for years, its mileage all untravelled, its power unused.

Too often older people are treated like the Ford in that story. We are patronized, kept in the parlour, polished and played with, but never taken out on the roads of life. Lutheran theologian Joseph Sittler called the way older people are patronized and treated like children 'geriatric shuffleboard'.

Like Hobab in the biblical story, we do not want to be coddled and treated as helpless children. We want to be challenged, to use our experience for the good of others. We want to be of service, to feel useful as long as we live.

Too often the church falls into the trap of believing that all older people want is fun and games. Too many activities focus on what author Maggie Kuhn called 'playpens for the elderly'. Like Moses' father-in-law, we often respond more to challenge than to entertaining games. We want to be used, not refused or abused.

REFLECTION

Instead of always thinking about what society can give us—our entitlements—let us look for ways we can give our talents back to society.

23

NUMBERS 13:3—14:10

AGEING'S ADVANCE SCOUT PARTY

But Caleb quieted the people before Moses, and said, 'Let us go up at once and occupy it, for we are well able to overcome it.' Then the men who had gone up with him said, 'We are not able to go up against this people, for they are stronger than we.' ... And Joshua son of Nun and Caleb son of Jephunneh... said to all the congregation of the Israelites, 'The land that we went through as spies is an exceedingly good land.'

Twelve spies were sent into Canaan to check it out and to bring back an advance scout report to Moses and the Israelites. The majority report (ten spies) terrified the Israelites with reports of fortified cities and gigantic peoples. They complained that they were 'like grasshoppers' in comparison to the Canaanites.

The minority report (Joshua and Caleb) advised Moses and the people to attack immediately, for, despite the obstacles, God would give them the land. They reacted in faith rather than fear. Regrettably, the people agreed with the majority report, and wandered forty more years in the wilderness.

Author Ram Dass claims that his role is as 'an advance scout of ageing'. He suffered a severe stroke, and knew some of the serious issues ageing brings, but he reported 'good news': the spirit is more powerful than the vicissitudes. 'Faith and love are stronger than any changes, stronger than ageing, and, I am very sure, stronger than death.'[6]

Ageing does bring inevitable losses and pains. It is neither the best of times nor the worst of times, but a special time that combines them both. We have more time and yet less time; we are more liberated and yet more limited. Things come together and things fall apart.

We can buy into the 'majority report' often heard in our society that ageing is a dreadful time because we face giants that make us seem 'like grasshoppers'. We can view ageing as shipwreck, chaos and something to dread. Or we can accept the 'minority report' of advance scouts, and know that despite the challenges we will face, it can be a good time.

The basic difference between Caleb and Joshua and the other advance scouts was that Caleb and Joshua trusted God. So, may God be with us as we face our ageing. I recall a placard that hung in my father's study: it read, 'One with God is a majority.'

PRAYER

God of our lives, through all the circling years we have trusted in you. So, as old age creeps on us, may our faith prevail even when the odds are against us.

24

DEUTERONOMY 31:30—32:9

STABILITY IN A CHANGING WORLD

Then Moses recited the words of this song, to the very end, in the hearing of the whole assembly of Israel: '...The Rock, his work is perfect, and all his ways are just. A faithful God, without deceit, just and upright is he.'

Before Moses gave his final blessing to the children of Israel before his death, he recited the words of a song which was to be sung by all following generations. The song of Moses (Deuteronomy 31:30—32:47) contrasts the faithfulness of God with Israel's faithlessness.

God is likened to a rock, because he is a faithful God who can be trusted, as Moses recited his saving deeds in days of old. God had told them, 'You have stayed long enough at this mountain. Resume your journey' (Deuteronomy 1:6). So they stood on the brink of changing times, entering a strange land unlike the wilderness to which they had become accustomed. But they could rely on the steadfastness of God, who would be their anchor and refuge as they left the sacred mountain for unknown valleys.

So often, older people feel threatened by the changes in society. Their world is often shaken by future shock that can create insecurity and uncertainty. This is why older people often repeat the same stories. These stories are not the meaningless meandering of senseless old people. They are one way to find consistency and stability in a changing world. Something doesn't change: some stories remain.

So, for the believer, the stories of the constancy and reliability of God, the Rock of Ages, remain our refuge whatever changes may occur. The ringing words of the writer to the Hebrews give us assurance: 'Therefore, since we are receiving a kingdom that cannot be shaken, let us give thanks, by which we offer to God an acceptable worship with reverence and awe' (Hebrews 12:28).

REFLECTION

Meditate on the words of this hymn, as you remember the steadfastness of God in your own life.

O God, the Rock of Ages,
Who evermore hast been,
What time the tempest rages,
Our dwelling place serene:
Before Thy first creations,
O Lord, the same as now,
To endless generations
The Everlasting Thou!

EDWARD H. BICKERSTETH (1825–1906)

25

Deuteronomy 34:1–8

It doesn't seem fair

Then Moses went up from the plains of Moab to Mount Nebo, to the top of Pisgah, which is opposite Jericho, and the Lord showed him the whole land… The Lord said to him, 'This is the land of which I swore to Abraham, to Isaac, and to Jacob, saying, 'I will give it to your descendants'; I have let you see it with your eyes, but you shall not cross over there.' Then Moses, the servant of the Lord, died there in the land of Moab.

It just doesn't seem fair, does it? Moses had completed all the course requirements, but God let him die on the mountain without graduating. If ever anyone deserved to enter the promised land, it was this powerful and passionate prophet of God. But Moses never realized his dream in his lifetime. As his clear eyes scanned the horizon and saw all the promised land, as far as the Western Sea, he had to feel some despair that his dream would be denied and his inheritance never collected. We cannot but feel sadness as he died in a lonely place on the mountain, his burial place a mystery, with no shaft of stones or grave marker. Yet we take comfort in the realization that the soul of Moses found shelter in God's presence and was swept away into eternity.

In the last sermon that Martin Luther King Jr preached in Memphis, Tennessee, he had premonitions about his death, and even likened that moment to the story of Moses' death. He died with his dream of racial justice delayed, although he knew that one day people would not be judged by the colour of their skin but by the content of their character.

What does this strange ending of Moses' life say to us? We may never realize our dreams in this life either. We may die with dreams denied, hope deferred and our inheritance not collected.

But wait a minute. There is another time, another mountain. Jesus took Peter, James and John to Mount Hermon, and to their amazed eyes, 'suddenly there appeared to them Moses and Elijah, talking with him' (Matthew 17:3). In the next world, Moses realized his dream, and did enter the promised land.

We will not realize all our hopes and dreams in this life, for 'a sabbath rest still remains for the people of God' (Hebrews 4:9). God's justice will not be denied. Moses was vindicated, and so will all of God's people be sustained.

PRAYER

God of the Ages, give me the assurance that this life is not the end, but that there is another life where our broken dreams come true.

26

JOSHUA 4:1–24 (NIV)

THE IMPORTANCE OF TRUSTED OBJECTS

So the Israelites did as Joshua commanded them. They took twelve stones from the middle of the Jordan, according to the number of the tribes of the Israelites, as the Lord had told Joshua; and they carried them over with them to their camp, where they put them down. Joshua set up the twelve stones… And they are there to this day.

There were two traditions preserved about memorial stones set up to commemorate the crossing of the Jordan by the Israelites. One describes the memorial stones set up at Gilgal; the other describes the stones set up in the bed of the river.

It seems more likely that the stones were set up in Gilgal in a circle, so that when future generations saw these stones, they would realize that God had brought their ancestors safely across the Jordan and set them in the land of promise. The circle of stones was symbolic of God's encircling love and care.

Many older people depend upon trusted objects, familiar signposts and daily routines when everything else falls away.

This is especially true of people who experience the mild dementia of Parkinson's or early Alzheimer's disease.

When older relatives have to enter nursing homes, they can take little of their former lives into the new space. Now their existence is limited to a room, or part of a room, with little space for all the mementos of their homes.

But some trusted objects need to be with them as they find themselves in unfamiliar territory. For some it might be faded wedding pictures or other photos of their past. For others it could be an old chair, reminiscent of comfort spent there, or a rug, or a picture of home, or old books, or sewing baskets. All remind us of who we were... and are.

Every time I visited an older lady from our parish, she would always clutch her time-worn Bible. 'I had many books in my library at home,' she said, 'but this is the book I always come back to now. It is my rock and my fortress.'

Indeed, like the stones at Gilgal, her Bible had sacramental overtones. The wonderful words of life in the Book encircled her with strength and hope, and reminded her that God would not leave her, but would go with her to the end.

REFLECTION

What sacred objects would *you* take with you if you had to leave your home and go to a nursing home or sheltered housing?

27

JOSHUA 14:6–25 (NJB)

CALEB: THE BIBLE'S LATE BLOOMER

'And now I am eighty-five years old. Today I am still as strong as the day when Moses sent me out on that errand; for fighting, for going and coming, I am as strong now as then. It is time you gave me the highlands, of which Yahweh spoke to me that day.'

Eighty-five-year-old Caleb is no shrinking violet. He is the Bible's classic late bloomer. At a time when the ease and comfort of retirement loomed before him, he was ready to face the giants of the mountain. He claimed the promised hill country and stood ready to fight for his rights. Only Joshua and Caleb had shown faith in God, when they were sent to spy out the land of Canaan. They believed when the others doubted, and the people rebelled. Then Caleb was much younger, forty years old. Now, 45 years later, he claimed the promise God made to him. His bold assertiveness was a clear demonstration of how God keeps promises to those who are faithful, at any age.

Caleb asserted, 'I wholeheartedly followed the Lord my God' (Joshua 14:8), and God affirmed that faith as recorded in the book of Numbers: 'But my servant Caleb... has a different spirit' (Numbers 14:24). Caleb was not too old to claim the promise, nor, despite his advanced years, did he lack the strength to fight.

Cicero wrote these words a hundred years before Christ: 'I am in my eighty-fourth year and... can say this much: that while I am not now, indeed, possessed of that physical strength which I had as a private soldier... old age has not quite unnerved or shattered me.'[7]

Caleb is a great role model for older people today. We need to claim our rights without apology. As long as we are able, we need to be in charge of our own lives, rather than passively letting outside forces control us. Some of the ageist terms are an affront to most older people. We are not 'old age pensioners' or 'golden oldies', but the elders, the experienced ones, who have rights that no one can deny. As long as our strength permits, we are a force with which to be reckoned.

A PRAYER FOR CALEB... AND HIS SUCCESSORS
Help us to show the strength of our years as did Caleb of old. May no one discount or discredit us because of our age.

28

RUTH 1:6–18

CARING FOR AN AGEING RELATIVE

So she said, 'See, your sister-in-law has gone back to her people and to her gods; return after your sister-in-law.' But Ruth said, 'Do not press me to leave you or to turn back from following you! Where you go, I will go; where you lodge, I will lodge; your people shall be my people, and your God my God. Where you die, I will die—there will I be buried. May the Lord do thus and so to me, more as well, if even death parts me from you!'

How unfortunate that the original context of Ruth's words have often been misconstrued. These were not vows expressed between husband and wife, but represent a commitment of a daughter-in-law to care for her ageing mother-in-law.

Caring for Naomi would not be an easy task. Bitterly complaining, she even asked to be called 'Bitter' (Mara), not 'Pleasant' (Naomi). Of course, you can't blame her. She left her homeland for a foreign country, and then watched her husband die. Within a space of ten years, two sons died. She became a poverty-stricken widow, and blamed God: 'The hand of the Lord has turned against me' (Ruth 1:13).

Ruth had every right and reason to stay in Moab, her home country. Her chances for another marriage were infinitely greater there than in a country where she would be a foreigner. But she cared for Naomi, and her loyalty went way beyond all the demands of duty. Unlike her sister Orpah who kissed Naomi and left, Ruth clung to her and promised to care for her until death parted them.

According to the population planning for the period between 1985 and 2025, it is predicted that over the next 25 years the number of older people aged 85 and older will double. Frailty and illness mean that this group is most likely to be in need of care.

Added to this is the decrease in the number of hospital beds and places in local authority residential homes. More and more people will have to stay at home, and the burden of responsibility will fall on the family. At first the commitment to care for an ageing relative may seem to be a way to pay back somehow all that the parent or spouse has given in the past. Yet, the strain is enormous.

However great the cost, nothing gives greater joy than caring for ageing relatives, being there for them whether at home or in a hospital or nursing home. There is simply no substitute for the kind of constant, unconditional care that Ruth gave Naomi.

PRAYER
Lord, if I am called on to care for an ageing relative, grant me wisdom, courage and strength.

29

RUTH 4:13–21

GRANDCHILDREN RENEW OUR LIVES

Then the women said to Naomi, 'Blessed be the Lord, who has not left you this day without next-of-kin… He shall be to you a restorer of life and a nourisher of your old age… Then Naomi took the child and laid him in her bosom, and became his nurse… They named him Obed; he became the father of Jesse, the father of David.

Naomi's bitterness is now at an end. She is comforted by the birth of a grandson, Obed, who shall be for her 'a restorer of life and a nourisher of… old age'. This child not only assured the future of her family name, but became the grandfather of King David and later an ancestor of Jesus, the Messiah. As she nursed little Obed, she felt her life renewed and restored. Obed helped Naomi to experience holy timelessness, for every time a grandchild is born, a grandparent is reborn!

We are blessed with ten grandchildren, and their antics constantly amuse us. Their presence evokes deep and mysterious feelings and that needed spark of joy when life can become tedious and routine.

When Daniel was four, he came with his family to eat lunch at a retirement community where I was delivering lectures. He seemed overwhelmed by all the old, white-haired people and blurted out, 'I never saw so many grandpas and grandmas in my life.' I wanted to crawl under a table, but the residents got a much-needed laugh.

My granddaughter, Kaitlyn, sitting in the back seat of a car, stared at my white hair and exclaimed, 'Grandpa, you don't wear that white hair to church, do you?' When I told her that I did, she retorted, 'If I were you, I'd get a wig!'

The story of Ruth and Obed not only points to the joy that grandchildren offer, but to the responsibility that grandparents have for these children. Parents may be gateways to the relationships between generations, but it's the grandparents' responsibility to keep the gate oiled. Our constant support, unconditional love and kind counsel provide solid foundations for these children. No wonder the ancient psalmist prayed, 'May you see your children's children' (Psalm 128:6). May that be our prayer, too.

PRAYER
Help us, loving Grandparent, to show the love and acceptance for our grandchildren that will brighten their days and encourage them for ever.

30

1 SAMUEL 3:1–10

MENTORING THE NEXT GENERATION

Now the boy Samuel was ministering to the Lord under Eli… At that time Eli, whose eyesight had begun to grow dim so that he could not see, was lying down in his room… Then Eli perceived that the Lord was calling the boy. Therefore Eli said to Samuel, 'Go, lie down; and if he calls you, you shall say, "Speak, Lord, for your servant is listening."'

It is true that we have natural children and spiritual children. Old Eli's natural sons, Phinehas and Hophni, were great disappointments. They were not only disobedient but their greed and sexual immorality created a public scandal. However, Eli's spiritual son, Samuel, was a true servant of God.

Eli had reached the age with nothing significant to do. He was almost blind and his strength was failing. He still held the important position as priest at Shiloh, yet he could not control his own sons. During these days and nights of serving in the temple, he must have felt some guilt over how he had failed as a father. And that is why Samuel meant so much to him, for unlike his sons, Samuel was well liked by all the Israelite worshippers who came to Shiloh.

Eli saw the leadership potential in the young Samuel and so he mentored him, providing the role model that the boy needed, passing on the flame of his wisdom. We find a great example of that modelling on a memorable night when God spoke to Samuel. Samuel thought it was Eli who called in the night, but Eli told him to be still and listen. Eli didn't identify the voice or the message, but simply told Samuel to listen, although Eli perceived that it was the Lord speaking to Samuel. The lamp of God burned all night (Leviticus 6:9), so it was just before dawn that Samuel heard God's call. Later Samuel became Israel's leader, providing stability, comfort and reassurance in the dark days that lay ahead.

Mentors are needed for the younger generation, to act as spiritual midwives, enabling the younger generation to find their own meaning. Many examples can be cited of older persons who serve as mentors and counsellors for the younger generation, and thus provide the bridge over which they walk to their future.

REFLECTION

Consider a younger person you know who might appreciate your counsel and wisdom. Be intentional about being available to him or her.

31

2 SAMUEL 18:24–33

AN AGED FATHER'S GRIEF

The king said to the Cushite, 'Is it well with the young man Absalom?' The Cushite answered, 'May the enemies of my lord the king, and all who rise up to do you harm, be like that young man.' The king was deeply moved, and went up to the chamber over the gate, and wept; and as he went, he said, 'O my son Absalom, my son, my son Absalom! Would I had died instead of you, O Absalom, my son, my son!'

As Jacob favoured Joseph, so David favoured Absalom. It seemed as if King David was always spoiling him. A thorn in David's flesh, Absalom was still the apple of his eye.

'Absalom stole the hearts of the people of Israel' (2 Samuel 15:6). Taking advantage of his natural appeal and charisma, he attempted to seize the throne from his father. After being formally anointed as king, he crossed the Jordan to meet his father's force in a decisive struggle for control of the throne.

While he awaited word from the battlefield, David was a wreck. If he was afraid he might lose his throne, he was even more afraid he might lose Absalom.

When the Cushite brought the news of Absalom's death, David's heart broke, and he cried out in words that have echoed down the centuries ever since, 'O Absalom, my son, my son! Would that I had died instead of you.' David regained his throne, but he never forgot his son, Absalom. Joab brought David to his senses and made him realize he was putting his personal grief above the welfare of Israel. David may have suppressed his grief but it did not end.

Sometimes we forget the pain of ageing parents when their children die. I recall visiting a 96-year-old mother whose 74-year-old son had died. Although he had lived a long life, she still grieved the loss of her son, and said, 'I just don't understand why I outlived him.'

REFLECTION

As you meditate on Bernard of Clairvaux's words on the cruxifixion, consider the grief of the Father God at the death of his beloved son.

> O sacred head, now wounded,
> With grief and shame weighed down;
> Now scornfully surrounded
> With thorns, Thine only crown.
> O sacred head, what glory
> What bliss till now was Thine!
> Yet though despised and gory,
> I joy to call Thee mine.

BERNARD OF CLAIRVAUX (1091–1153)

32

2 SAMUEL 19:31–40

BARZILLAI: A MAN WHO ACCEPTED HIS AGEING

Barzillai was a very aged man, eighty years old… The king said to Barzillai, 'Come over with me, and I will provide for you in Jerusalem at my side.' But Barzillai said to the king, 'How many years have I still to live, that I should go up with the king to Jerusalem? … Why then should your servant be an added burden to my lord the king?

Barzillai, a man of wealth, had come to King David's support in a crucial moment. Other friends deserted David when his son, Absalom, tried to seize the throne. David's assets were frozen in Jerusalem and he needed supplies, so Barzillai chipped in with a large donation.

When he was restored to power, David offered Barzillai a political perk. He invited him to return with him, live in Jerusalem as his permanent guest, and be cared for while he lived out his days on earth.

Barzillai did not want to offend the king and so refused his offer, listing many of the frailties of his advanced age. Faltering mental alertness, lack of appetite, and poor hearing and vision would make him a burden to the king. He preferred to return to his familiar haunts and spend his later years in Gilead, where his parents were buried.

Barzillai is a symbol of those many older people who give generously to God's work. When several older members in an Episcopal parish died, the rector said, 'I have buried half my Sunday's collection in the past months. We will miss their financial commitment to the church.' Large bequests and generous gifts from older church members indicate their commitment and their determination to keep the work of the church not only solvent but strong.

Barzillai also represents the strong feeling of most older people that they do not want to be burdens to their families. They are quite aware of their frailties and diminishments, but they do not want to add further burdens to their children's lives. Maintaining their independence, determining their own destinies, is one of the final dignities that exists for older people.

David seemed to respect Barzillai's request and did not try to dissuade him from his choice. David affirmed his right to be independent, and gave him the freedom of his choice.

PRAYER
We thank you, O Lord, for all older people whose support for the church goes beyond the second mile.

33

2 SAMUEL 21:1–14

THE RIZPAH VIGIL

The king took the two sons of Rizpah daughter of Aiah… Armoni and Mephibosheth… [and] gave them into the hands of the Gibeonites, and they impaled them on the mountain before the Lord… Then Rizpah… took sackcloth, and spread it on a rock for herself… she did not allow the birds of the air to come upon the bodies by day, or the wild animals by night.

Rizpah is a good example of the undying love of a mother. The concubine of Saul, her two sons were hanged during a famine in David's reign. In seeking a reason for the famine, David concluded that it was because of Saul's attempt to wipe out the Gibeonites, and sentenced seven sons or grandsons of Saul (including the sons of Rizpah) to death.

For five months, from the barley harvest until the early rains, Rizpah watched over the dead, unburied bodies of her two sons. What a ghastly scene that must have been, watching her sons' broken bodies gradually decay, vigilantly protecting them from the vultures.

Rizpah spread sackcloth on the rock, a symbol associated not only with mourning but also with the public expression of humiliation and penitence. She defended her dead until the rain came—a sign that God had withdrawn his judgment.

King David was moved by her devotion and finally gave the dead men an honourable burial as soon as the rains fell. Rizpah's loving vigil helped to protect her sons' bodies from desecration and dishonour.

David ordered that the uncared-for bones of Saul and Jonathan, which still lay at Jabesh-Gilead, be recovered. Apparently their bones were mingled with the bones of Rizpah's sons and Saul's grandsons in the family grave at Zelah.

Some writers have drawn attention to the similarities between Rizpah, as she stood by seven trees on the hillside, and Mary and the other women who stood by the tree where Christ was hanged. No doubt, in that 'mountain before the Lord' (2 Samuel 21:9) we have a shadow of Golgotha. Rizpah could not forget the sons of her love, and her sacrificial vigil of dead became a symbol of perpetual devotion. Rizpah, in her suffering, typifies thousands of care-givers who are sitting by the bedside of suffering loved ones or mourning their death.

REFLECTION
Think when you may have sat at the bedside of a loved one, either sick or dying. What were your feelings? What regrets? How were you aware of God's presence then?

34

1 Kings 1:1–4 (NIV)

Care-giving for an old king

When King David was old and well advanced in years, he could not keep warm even when they put covers over him. So his servants said to him, 'Let us look for a young virgin to attend the king and take care of him…' Then they searched throughout Israel for a beautiful girl and found Abishag, a Shunammite, and brought her to the king… She took care of the king and waited on him, but the king had no intimate relations with her.

A sad scene for the old king. The man had had nine wives and many mistresses—but none was present to care for him in his old age. The virile, charismatic king, whose passionate nature had wooed many women and won the hearts of Israel, now faced old age cold and alone. Not even the bedcovers could fend off the ominous chill he felt in his bones.

The endless stories of David's sexual exploits were now forgotten, as all that remained was a shivering old king, needing someone to care for him. The fires of life were almost all out, and in order to rekindle them and save their own jobs, his advisors enlisted the aid of a young woman named Abishag. Perhaps they believed that a young virgin would have miraculous powers to cure senility and revive the impotent king.

Although she cared for the old king, he died soon thereafter. When Adonijah offered to make an honest woman of Abishag by marrying her, the Solomon coalition got rid of him. Apparently they believed that taking over his father's care-giver was taking over his father's throne.

One interesting question is, 'Where were all of David's children?' Why were they not involved in their ageing father's care? We do not know why their absence is so obvious.

There comes a time when family and close friends cannot bear the burden. Although we can fill some of our parents' needs easily and without too much distress, others we cannot. There is no way adult children can fill the gap in parents' lives that result from loss of valued friends and family. We cannot cure our parents' depressions, or protect them from every risk. We cannot give the kind of constant care they may demand.

Abishag appears for only a brief moment on the stage of biblical history, but she reminds us of known and unknown care-givers who make our ageing lives less stressful.

PRAYER

Holy One, when I am able to give care, let me do it wholly and with love. Help me also to rest and, when I feel guilty, to remember Jesus' words, 'Draw away, and rest a while.' Help me turn over the care to others.

35

THE PERIL OF REJECTING OLD PEOPLE

Then King Rehoboam took counsel with the older men who had attended his father Solomon while he was still alive, saying, 'How do you advise me to answer this people?' They answered him, 'If you will be a servant to this people today and serve them, and speak good words to them when you answer them, then they will be your servants for ever.' But he disregarded the advice that the older men gave him, and consulted with the young men.

Author Malcolm Cowley once wrote, 'To enter the country of age is a new experience, different from what you supposed it to be. Nobody, man or woman, knows the country until he has lived in it and has taken out his citizenship papers.'[8] Apparently the young King Rehoboam had no understanding of the wisdom of the elders.

When Jeroboam and the whole congregation of Israel asked Rehoboam to lighten up and free them from the burdensome policies of Solomon, Rehoboam asked the elders for their advice. They counselled compassion and a relaxation of the oppressive policies of Solomon.

Instead, Rehoboam took the recommendations of the young hot-heads who felt that any hint of compromise would be interpreted as a sign of impotence. So Rehoboam shut his ears to the old and listened to the young, threatening even more severity and servitude.

By not listening to the wisdom of the elders, Rehoboam plunged the nation into a senseless civil war. In this instance, the counsel of the old was unquestionable wisdom.

Despite the folly of the young men in this story, there is no doubt that generations need each other. Psychologist Mary Pipher points out that before the pioneers came, the Native Americans of the Great Plains survived the harsh winters by having grandparents and grandchildren sleep beside each other. That kept both generations from freezing to death. She writes, 'That is a good metaphor for what the generations do for each other. We keep each other from freezing. The old need our heat, and we need their light.'[9]

Rehoboam should have listened to the 'light' that his elders offered. What might have happened if he had regarded the wisdom of the older men and listened to their counsel? We simply cannot afford to consign older persons to the scrapheap of history, for they have been through enough battles to know what life is all about.

PRAYER

Help us, O wise God, to listen to those who have long journeyed the well-travelled roads, and who know from experience the perils and pitfalls.

36

ELIJAH AND THE OUTCAST WIDOW

So [Elijah] set out and went to Zarephath. When he came to the gate of the town, a widow was there gathering sticks; he called to her and said, 'Bring me a little water in a vessel, so that I may drink.' As she was going to bring it, he called to her and said, 'Bring me a morsel of bread in your hand.' … She went and did as Elijah said, so that she as well as he and her household ate for many days.

I am increasingly drawn to the story of this unnamed widow, who lived in Zarephath on the Phoenician coast. Elijah spotted her gathering sticks for firewood and asked for her water and bread. The woman wanted to be hospitable, but asking for bread was a little too much.

She told Elijah that she was gathering wood to bake the handful of meal and bit of oil that were left for herself and her son, and that they would eat this meal and await death.

Elijah reassured her: 'Fear not,' he said. 'Make me a little cake anyway, and afterwards feed yourself and your son.' She went and did as Elijah said, and was amazed that the jar of meal was not emptied, neither did the jug of oil fail.

Why is this story in the Bible? It is a strange story of a

woman about to die with her son, a mother unable to feed her little boy, yet who still responded to the need of a neighbour. Later at Mount Carmel, Elijah would call down fire in dramatic fashion to consume the lumber.

The story of a poor widow setting fire to a few sticks in order to cook a little cake seems to pale in significance. But it *is* a great story. Remember, the widow is a Gentile outcast, and it is remarkable that Elijah would ask her for anything.

This story of God's inclusive love and compassion is recalled by Jesus in his first sermon in the synagogue at Nazareth. He reminded his Hebrew audience of their own history. There were many widows in Israel in the days of Elijah, 'but to none of them was Elijah sent except to Zarephath… to a woman who was a widow' (Luke 4:26, NKJV).

For Elijah and Jesus, human need knew no boundaries, and their compassion for the widow is testimony of God's love for outcasts. In societies which exclude outsiders, these stories remind us that 'the love of God is broader than the measure of man's mind, and the heart of the Eternal is most wonderfully kind' (Frederick William Faber).

REFLECTION

Can you recall moments when outsiders extended a helping hand? How can older people relate to this story?

37

2 KINGS 2:9–15 (NIV)

WHEN THE MENTOR LEAVES

When they had crossed, Elijah said to Elisha, 'Tell me, what can I do for you before I am taken from you?' 'Let me inherit a double portion of your spirit,' Elisha replied… [Elisha] picked up the cloak that had fallen from Elijah and went back and stood on the bank of the Jordan.

Throughout the Old Testament, mentors used their experience, wisdom and resources to come alongside younger, less experienced men or women to help them mature. Jethro, Moses' father-in-law, mentored Moses on how to shepherd the sheep, and later counselled him to appoint leaders to help in the administration of Israel.

Elijah had mentored Elisha, and now the time had come for Elijah to pass the torch to his successor. So, nearing the end of life, Elijah passed the prophetic mantle to his student Elisha, who would take his place as prophet to the people of Israel. Elisha would be recognized as Elijah's legitimate successor by being given a double portion of his spirit. After Elijah was taken to heaven, Elisha put on Elijah's mantle and assumed a leadership role.

Anticipating the end of one's life and work is not always

easy to accept, but it must be faced and plans made to pass control and authority to the next generation. If this is done well, the transition can be a positive experience. Done poorly, conflict around issues of control can ensue.

If you work on a computer for an hour and there is a power failure, that work can disappear from the computer's memory. Similarly, if older persons don't 'save' their life experience through mentoring and through leaving legacies, that wisdom can disappear from memory.

We know the importance of making a will in case of death or incapacity. We need to take the same care in making an ethical will, ensuring that our spiritual heritage is also passed on to the next generation.

Elijah mentored Elisha and passed the torch of leadership to him, and Israel still heard the voice of the prophet. Now, as the older generation leaves the scene, will the new generation remember our values and virtues?

PRAYER

Grant, O God, that if we are older we may hand on our values to the next generations, and if we are younger we may ask for them.

38

2 Kings 2:9–12

Coping with major losses

As they continued walking and talking, a chariot of fire and horses of fire separated the two of them, and Elijah ascended in a whirlwind into heaven. Elisha kept watching and crying out, 'Father, father! The chariots of Israel and its horsemen!'

John was my mentor, a trusted friend whose experience in the ministry had always been a source of wisdom to everyone. His death was sudden and swift. Racing to baptize a dying child, he had a major stroke and crashed into another car, and his life ended several hours later. A few months earlier we had celebrated his ministry, and I can still hear him quoting the words of Tennyson from 'Ulysses': 'Death closes all: but something ere the end, some work of noble note, may yet be done.' John's life was a 'work of noble note'.

Hidden away in 2 Kings is the story of the day God took Elijah up to heaven. Elisha was his student, and he always called Elijah 'Father'. Elijah was not his actual father, but Elisha felt like his son. So, when Elijah was taken to heaven, Elisha cried and mourned his loss.

The death of those to whom we are close always affects our lives. We become diminished when our friends and mentors die. As the years increase, we lose more and more of those who have been our friends and graced our lives. Our world has grown smaller and lonelier, and we are left without their graceful presence.

Elisha took up the mantle that had fallen from Elijah and put it on his shoulders, and he went back to the banks of the Jordan. He did not forget his father, nor did he grieve for ever. He asked for the spirit of Elijah, and received it.

It was hard to give up my old friend, John. Not a week passes that I don't remember him and relive memories of our friendship. John was an elder who had synthesized wisdom from a long experience in the ministry and transformed it into a legacy. Saying goodbye to him was difficult, but it meant saying hello to new challenges to carry on his ministry.

REFLECTION

Write your name in the centre of a circle and imagine yourself sitting in the centre of a circle of light. Imagine significant persons in your life who have died, standing at the circumference of the circle. You look at them and want to thank them for their presence in your life.

39

ISAIAH 6:1–8 (NJB)

WHEN AN OLD KING DIES

In the year of King Uzziah's death I saw the Lord seated on a high and lofty throne… Then I said: 'Woe is me! I am lost, for I am a man of unclean lips and I live among a people of unclean lips, and my eyes have seen the King, Yahweh Sabaoth.'

Isaiah had fled to the temple in an hour of great tragedy and impending doom for his nation. The old king, Uzziah, was dead, and it seemed to signal the end of the nation, the tragic wreckage of all his hopes and dreams.

King Uzziah ascended the throne aged 16 and reigned longer than any previous king in Israel or Judah—52 years. A wise, pious and powerful king, he extended Judah's territory and brought the nation to a time of great prosperity.

However, near the end of his reign, he was no longer satisfied to be a mortal king, but wanted to be a divine king. He entered the temple to burn incense and was stricken with leprosy. His final days were spent in seclusion, with his son, Jotham, probably acting as king.

His death at the age of 68 was still a shock to Isaiah—'As when a lordly cedar, green with boughs, goes down with a great shout upon the hills, and leaves a lonesome place against the sky'.[10]

In that hour of personal loss, and the death of hope for his people, Isaiah saw the Lord. In the temple he met the living God whose glory filled the heavens and the earth. The earthly king was dead; his throne was vacant. But Isaiah encountered the Living King, Yahweh Saboath, whose throne was never vacant.

Isaiah's hero, Uzziah, had sinned late in life and died in shame. But the Lord God, the true King, was holy, the Wholly Other, whose presence brought a sense of glory, majesty and power that transformed Isaiah.

We all have our heroes and heroines, and sometimes it is only later that we realize their faults and failures. The words of the psalmist ring true: 'It is better to trust in the Lord than to put confidence in man. It is better to trust in the Lord than to put confidence in princes' (Psalm 118:8–9, NKJV).

At the death of the old king, Isaiah experienced *the* King, and his life was for ever changed.

PRAYER

Lord, forgive us for putting our ultimate trust in finite people and not in your infinite mercy.

40

Psalm 46

Learning to be Still

God is our refuge and strength, a very present help in trouble. Therefore we will not fear, though the earth should change… 'Be still, and know that I am God! I am exalted among the nations, I am exalted in the earth.' The Lord of hosts is with us; the God of Jacob is our refuge.

The invincible army of Sennacherib which had swept across the Fertile Crescent stood outside the gates of Jerusalem. Hezekiah, the king, was shut up like a bird in a cage, terrified that the end had come for Judah. The Rabshakeh (the Assyrian 'field commander', NIV) had taunted the frightened people with his arrogant bluster and tempted them to capitulate. But Isaiah counselled the king to take heart, be still and trust God (Isaiah 36—37).

It seems as if Psalm 46 could well have been written by Isaiah to describe this moment of holy history. 'The nations raged, the kingdoms were moved' (v. 6, NKJV), and it seemed as if Judah's fate was doomed. Yet Isaiah counselled Hezekiah and the people, 'Be still and know that I am God' (v. 10). Don't panic. Don't do anything. Just trust.

When we experience any threats to our lives, we tend to

become anxious and almost panicky. Silent trust in God is needed. Yet silent trust is a rare commodity in our noisy culture. Silence is seen as some kind of deviant behaviour. Even in the church we find noise and hurry, climb, push and shove. Blaise Pascal once wrote, 'I have often said that the sole cause of man's unhappiness is that he does not know how to stay quietly in his room' (*Pensées* 139).

Earlier Isaiah had counselled, 'In returning and rest you shall be saved; in quietness and confidence shall be your strength' (Isaiah 30:15, NKJV). Now, in this hour when all seemed lost, the answer was in quiet confidence that God was in control.

When we are threatened by all that old age can bring, we need the quiet confidence that centres our souls in the midst of strife. Judah was delivered from Assyria. The nation escaped destruction. At times we will be delivered, too; at times we will not. But whatever comes to us, we need the quiet confidence that 'the Lord of hosts is with us; the God of Jacob is our refuge'.

PRAYER

Drop thy still dews of quietness,
Till all our strivings cease;
Take from our souls the strain and stress,
And let our ordered lives confess
The beauty of thy peace.

JOHN GREENLEAF WHITTIER (1807–92)

41

ISAIAH 38:1—39:8 (NKJV)

SAVED AT DEATH'S DOOR

*In those days Hezekiah was sick and near death. And Isaiah the
prophet, the son of Amoz, went to him and said to him, 'Thus
says the Lord: "Set your house in order, for you shall die and not
live."' Then Hezekiah turned his face toward the wall, and
prayed to the Lord... Then the word of the Lord came... 'I have
heard your prayer, I have seen your tears; and I will add to your
days fifteen years.'*

King Hezekiah, who had seen Jerusalem saved from certain
destruction, now faced his own death. When Isaiah the
prophet told the king to 'put his house in order' because he
would not recover from his illness, Hezekiah prayed for
deliverance. God heard his prayer, healed his disease and
prolonged his life by fifteen years. The sun's shadow moving
backward by ten degrees on the sundial of Ahaz was a symbol
of Hezekiah's extended time (Isaiah 38:8).

In these days of medical wonders, it is incredible how many
people, seemingly at the door of death, recover to live fifteen
or more years. We all know older people for whom there
seemed no future, and we had given them up, only to see
them restored by medical science. We are blessed with bonus

years beyond what seemed our end. So many older people are like Jonah, spat back into life by the great fish of illness. Medical technology keeps enlarging the numbers of older people who live normally in remission. Indeed, there seems to be a new remission society in our time of older people who have survived critical illnesses.

After his earlier prayer for healing had been answered, Hezekiah, like the one leper who returned to thank Jesus, gave thanks. He wrote, '[God] himself has done this… Lord, by such things men live; and my spirit finds life in them too. You restored me to health and let me live' (Isaiah 38:15–16, NIV). Hezekiah discovered that it was Yahweh who had restored him to health, and never forgot that time when his life got out of focus. He knew that fifteen years longer to live was a pure gift.

For those, like Hezekiah, who belong to the 'remission society', the sun also rises on a world that is a new day in all its opportunity and danger.

PRAYER
God of health, when you restore us from illness and give us more years to live, grant that we may never forget when life got out of focus, and may now serve you with new passion.

42

2 KINGS 22:3–20 (NKJV)

THE BOOK WE ALWAYS
COME BACK TO

*Then Hilkiah the high priest said to Shaphan the scribe, 'I have
found the Book of the Law in the house of the Lord.' And Hilkiah
gave the book to Shaphan, and he read it… Then Shaphan the
scribe showed the king, saying, 'Hilkiah the priest has given me
a book.' And Shaphan read it before the king… So Hilkiah the
priest… went to Huldah the prophetess.*

I gave Miss Essie, the Assistant Food Director at our church, a
new large-print Bible. No one knows how old she really is, but
suffice it to say that she has walked the earth many moons.
With tears rolling down her cheeks, she fingered its pages and
said, 'I will read it every day and every night.' And she will.

When Hilkiah and Shaphan found a book buried somewhere in the temple, they weren't sure about the identity of
the scroll. Although it was an old book, it was as if they had
found a book they had never read. King Josiah recognized
the scroll as the words of Moses, and consulted with a
prophetess, Huldah, rather than Jeremiah. Huldah interpreted
the book to the king.

Older people are constantly rediscovering the Bible. John Bunyan, in *Grace Abounding*, tells how he read the Bible with new eyes: 'Indeed, I was then never out of the Bible.' Older people love the Bible. One 94-year-old woman, whose eyesight was growing dimmer every day, told me, 'I save whatever eyesight is left for the Bible. It is the only book I read where the author is always present!'

As the aged Sir Walter Scott lay dying, he asked that he might be wheeled into his library and placed before the window that commanded a beautiful view of the River Tweed. The famous author expressed the desire that his attendant read to him. 'But from what book?' the attendant asked, seeing that there were thousands of volumes in the library. 'Need you ask?' Sir Walter responded. 'There is but one.' So the attendant read to him from the 14th chapter of John.

The Bible is the book we always come back to—and, especially in the later years, we find it still the one irreplaceable book. It is indeed *the* treasure in earthen vessels.

MEDITATION
Holy Bible, Book Divine,
Precious treasure, thou art mine.
Mine to tell me whence I came;
Mine to teach me what I am.
Holy Bible, Book Divine,
Precious treasure, thou art mine.

WILLIAM B. BRADBURY (1816–68)

43

1 CHRONICLES 29:26–30

A GOOD OLD AGE

Thus David son of Jesse reigned over all Israel. The period that he reigned over Israel was forty years; he reigned seven years in Hebron, and thirty-three years in Jerusalem. He died in a good old age, full of days, riches, and honour.

With these words the chronicler ends the story of David. His had indeed been a great reign, and he died 'in a good old age, full of days, riches, and honour'.

An advertisement in London for a certain shoe polish shows an old but beautifully preserved pair of shoes, with the caption, 'They are well worn but they have worn well.' This describes King David, who had many battles in his life and yet died at the age of seventy, in a good old age.

Jean Vanier has said that there are two ways of growing old. There are old people who are shut away in their sadness and loneliness, living in the past and shrivelled up in themselves. On the other hand, there are older people with a child's heart, gentle and merciful, symbols of compassion and forgiveness. They are the community's true treasures.[11]

David surely was no paragon of virtue. His sin with Bathsheba led to dire consequences for himself, his family and the nation. He had feet of clay like the rest of us, if not more so—David was self-serving, lustful and hungry for power. Yet David was a man after God's own heart (1 Samuel 13:14). Faced with his sin, David repented and received God's forgiveness. It was David who united a divided kingdom, brought peace and prosperity to the nation and ushered in a golden age for Israel. His influence in the life of the nation was so great that God promised David a kingdom that would have no end.

As life reaches its end, how do we die 'in a good old age'? It is not a matter of power and wealth but of the quality of life we have lived. Seeking and doing the will of God, finding forgiveness for our transgressions and walking closely with God—these are the qualities that mark a good old age.

PRAYER

Grant, O living God, that we shall age with wisdom, compassion and grace now, so that, like David, we shall die in a good old age.

44

PSALM 72 (NIV)

OLD KING DAVID WROTE SOME PSALMS

Endow the king with your justice, O God, the royal son with your righteousness… Long may he live! … May people ever pray for him and bless him all day long… Praise be to the Lord God, the God of Israel, who alone does marvellous deeds. Praise be to his glorious name for ever; may the whole earth be filled with his glory. Amen and Amen.

James Ball Naylor wrote these rather humorous words:

> *King David and King Solomon*
> *Led merry, merry lives,*
> *With many, many lady friends*
> *And many, many wives.*
> *But when old age crept upon them*
> *With many, many qualms,*
> *King Solomon wrote the Proverbs*
> *and King David wrote the Psalms.*
>
> POEM

While we may chuckle at these words about David's full sense of the loss of sexual prowess, they are also a tribute to old King David. The last ten years of his life were no picnic. He survived the sad revolt of Absalom and Absalom's death, a three-year famine after his return to power, then the revolt of Adonijah.

But David did not hang up his harp. He wrote many of the psalms in his later years. In the Hebrew Bible, David's name occurs in 72 psalm titles. If David did not write all these psalms, at least there arose a tradition that connected David with them.

The 72nd Psalm is believed to be David's last psalm, prayed for his son, Solomon, as he ascended the throne. John Calvin believed that David uttered this prayer as he was dying, and that it was put into the form of a psalm by his son, Solomon, that the memory might never perish. If so, David dies exhorting Solomon to give God all the glory.

Monica Furlong wrote some words about ageing which seem to epitomize David's life: 'What I believe can redeem old age, as indeed the whole of life, is a passionate commitment to living as fully as possible, whatever the restrictions.'[12]

Despite his faults and failures, David displayed 'a passionate commitment to living as fully as possible', and ended his life with undying praise to the God of Israel. King Henry V left life saying, 'Laud be to God, even there shall my life end. Amen.'

PRAYER

Bless the Lord, O my soul, and all that is within me, bless his holy name. Bless the Lord, O my soul, and do not forget all his benefits (Psalm 103:1–2).

45

2 CHRONICLES 16:11–14

A MAGNIFICENT FUNERAL, BUT...?

Then Asa slept with his ancestors, dying in the forty-first year of his reign. They buried him in the tomb that he had hewn out for himself in the city of David; They laid him on a bier that had been filled with various kinds of spices prepared by the perfumer's art; and they made a very great fire in his honour.

She did not want a lavish funeral. Although one of the wealthiest persons in town, she requested a simple memorial service, and her remains were placed in a single niche in the columbarium outside her church. She did not want people to file past her coffin, wondering if her body looked good. Rather, she wanted those who came to the service to know that God is good. After a brief committal of her ashes in the memorial garden, the memorial service was a testimony to the simplicity and reality of her life.

How different the funeral of King Asa. The Chronicler tells us that 'Asa did what was good and right in the eyes of the Lord' (2 Chronicles 14:2). His religious reforms tore down pagan images and restored the temple altar. He was instrumental in getting the tribes of Judah and Benjamin to renew the covenant with God at Jerusalem. He was one of the four most godly kings in Judah, and reigned for 41 years.

In the 39th year of his reign, Asa contracted a disease in his feet and, two years later, died. His funeral rites were magnificent. He was buried in a tomb he had made for himself, filled with spices and ointments. The 'very great fire' of 16:14 refers to a ceremonial fire on which incense and spices were cast. No expense was spared to make his funeral a lavish occasion.

King Louis XIV was very specific in his will about the way he wanted his funeral to be conducted. The cathedral was to be dimly lit with one large candle placed next to the golden coffin. The king wanted a spectacular funeral that drew attention to *his* greatness. Bishop Massillon was appointed to give the eulogy. The large congregation waited in hushed silence. The bishop walked to the casket, reached up to the candle, snuffed it out and said, 'Only God is great!'

As we make plans for our own funeral, what will it say to those who assemble? Will it witness to the lavishness of our life, or the greatness and goodness of God?

REFLECTION

Spend a few moments of meditation on how you would plan your funeral.

46

2 CHRONICLES 23:1–12; 24:15–16

JEHOIADA: NEGLECTED VOICE OF THE STORY

But Jehoiada grew old and full of days, and died; he was one hundred and thirty years old at his death. And they buried him in the city of David among the kings, because he had done good in Israel, and for God and his house.

So many lives and stories of biblical characters represent neglected voices who are out of the spotlight. These characters, although often overlooked, play major roles in the biblical narrative. Such a lesser voice was the aged priest, Jehoiada, who lived to be 130 years.

His courageous act of hiding the young King Joash from the wrath of Queen Athaliah helped to preserve the line of David. After Joash became king, Jeohoiada was a powerful influence for good in the kingdom. Under his oversight, the temple of Baal was torn down and the influence of Baalism over the people was reduced. The temple of the Lord was then restored to its former glory (see 2 Chronicles 22:11; 23:16-24:14).

When he died, he was awarded the honour of being buried with kings, 'because he had done good in Israel, both for God and his house'. Jehoiada may well have been the only priest in Israel who was buried in a royal tomb.

Older persons today can contribute greatly in the margins of the church. Although their voices may be seldom heard in church and community, they may render quiet service behind the scenes. At times it is playing cameo roles, like old actors and actresses who play the role, then disappear. At other times they make their presence known in moments of decision or crisis, although they are far from the centres of power.

To live in the margins is not to live apart from God. Church workers and clergy, like Jehoiada, add depth and spiritual value, and deepen our sense of how God works behind the scenes, then and now. As John Milton said so well, 'Who best bear his mild yoke, they serve him best... They also serve who only stand and wait' ('On His Blindness').

PRAYER

We praise you, gracious God, for older people who keep the fires of faith burning in your churches, and whose nameless acts of kindness and mercy make the world a better place in which to live.

47

THE INFLUENCE OF A TRANSFORMED GRANDFATHER

While [Manasseh] was in distress he entreated the favour of the Lord his God and humbled himself greatly before the God of his ancestors. He prayed to him, and God received his entreaty, heard his plea, and restored him again to Jerusalem and to his kingdom. Then Manasseh knew that the Lord indeed was God.

If you read the story of the early reign of Manasseh (2 Chronicles 33:1 - 9), it is a sordid story of sin and rebellion. Reverting to the evil ways of his grandfather, Ahaz, he erected altars to Baal, worshipped the sun, moon and stars, and even sacrificed his own son to Molech. This king, who reigned 55 years, had the dubious distinction of being Judah's most wicked king, and was portrayed as an arch-villain in the most lurid light.

Later in his life, he repented and humbled himself before God. He then tried to reverse the trends he had established, and took away foreign gods and idols from the city. He even commanded Judah to worship the Lord God of Israel.

Manasseh became an exemplary king in his later years, and

proved that the power of repentance is so great that it can overshadow long years of sinful behaviour.

What intrigues me is the influence that Manasseh had on his grandson, Josiah. Manasseh's son, Amon, returned to the sinful ways of his father's earlier reign. Amon's servants murdered him and killed him in his own home. Manasseh's grandson, Josiah, became king when he was eight years old.

Apparently, grandfather Manasseh had a great influence on the young Josiah during the formative years of his life. Rather than perpetuating the wicked policies of his father, Amon, Josiah initiated happy years of peace, prosperity and reform in Judah. In the eighteenth year of his reign he instituted a great reform with the discovery of the Book of the Law.

Although Josiah may have been surrounded by God-fearing advisers, I like to think that Manasseh was the greatest influence on him and helped him to 'seek the God of his ancestor David' (2 Chronicles 34:3). Do not underestimate the influence that a grandparent may have on grandchildren: seeds are sown that bear fruit in later years.

PRAYER

Eternal God, turn our hearts to those grandparents whose faith touched our lives, and help us to hand down that same faith to our grandchildren.

CONFRONTED BY AN AGED UNCLE

Mordecai told them to reply to Esther, 'Do not think that in the king's palace you will escape any more than all the other Jews. For if you keep silence at such a time as this, relief and deliverance will rise for the Jews from another quarter, but you and your father's family will perish. Who knows? Perhaps you have come to royal dignity for just such a time as this.'

Esther could have played it safe (or so she thought). She had won the Persian beauty contest, and had it made as the king's favourite wife. But her uncle, Mordecai, made her struggle. Mordecai had adopted her when her parents died. Now his refusal to bow down and grovel in the dust before Haman, a raging anti-Semite, had led to the possibility that her people were be annihilated.

Mordecai reminded Esther that if she clung to her security in the king's palace, relief would come from another source, and she might perish. Instead, he told her that this was the moment for which she had been born. She had come 'to royal dignity for just such a time as this'.

Older people are constantly faced with places of risk, where we pause or teeter. Sometimes these difficulties are freely chosen and at other times they are thrust upon us.

We may be facing hard choices about relocating from our homes, or facing hip or knee replacements, using a walking frame, or surrendering our driving licence. We can either retreat to the safety of old securities, cling to the familiar ways, or take the bold leap to trust.

Esther chose to take the leap of faith. 'I will go to the king, though it is against the law; and if I perish, I perish' (v. 16). She put her life on the line and risked everything. With great tact and skill, Esther exposed Haman's plot and true character to the king. As a result, her people were delivered.

Although we praise the courage of Esther, we must not overlook the wisdom of Mordecai. He knew that Esther alone had the power to save the Jews, and he said the right words that spoke to her soul. This was one time that an older man's presence and words of challenge brought deliverance to God's people.

PRAYER

Give us the courage, O God, to listen and heed the words of those who make us surrender our security for growth.

49

ESTHER 6:1–3

GOD'S NIGHT SCHOOL

On that night the king could not sleep, and he gave orders to bring the book of records, the annals, and they were read to the king. It was found written how Mordecai had told about Bigthana and Teresh, two of the king's eunuchs, who guarded the threshold, and who had conspired to assassinate King Ahasuerus. Then the king said, 'What honour or distinction has been bestowed on Mordecai for this?'

Old King Ahasuerus suffered from insomnia, so on that sleepless night officials began to read the boring book of records to put him to sleep. In that book was recorded how Mordecai had unearthed the plot to assassinate the king. Ahasuerus belatedly and apparently accidentally came to recognize Mordecai's part in saving his life and the fact that the deed had gone unrewarded.

More than half the people over 65 complain about insomnia, but few recognize it as a spiritual opportunity. We toss and turn and hold regular 'worry' sessions in the small hours of the night. Plagued by anxiety and fears, it is easy to curse the darkness.

Morton Kelsey, the Episcopalian priest and author, told the

story that when he was a young priest he began to wake regularly in the middle of the night. He cried out to the Lord, 'Why is this happening to me?' And he heard the answer, 'Morton, you're so busy doing my work all day that this is the only time I can get your attention.'

Being alone with God in the middle of the night, when all distractions are far away, can be an opportunity to do some important spiritual work in our later years. The TV is switched off and the computer is still. It can be a time for forgiving others and asking forgiveness for ourselves. It may be a time of praying for others. I know older people in their 90s who pray for family, friends and church throughout the long, endless hours of the night.

Or, it may be a time when we learn simply to 'be' with God and to realize God's presence. When Jacob woke from his troubled sleep at Bethel, he exclaimed, 'Surely the Lord is in this place—and I did not know it!' (Genesis 28:16).

During that fretful, sleepless night when they read the book of the chronicles to the king, it became a grace moment, a meaningful moment in the story of Israel. So, our sleepless nights can become God's night school!

PRAYER

I will both lie down and sleep in peace; for you alone, O Lord, make me lie down in safety (Psalm 4:8).

50

JOB 2:11–13

JOB'S OLD FRIENDS

Now when Job's three friends heard of all these troubles that had come upon him, each of them set out from his home—Eliphaz the Temanite, Bildad the Shuhite, and Zophar the Naamathite. They met together to go and console and comfort him. When they saw him from a distance, they did not recognize him, and they raised their voices and wept aloud; they tore their robes and threw dust in the air upon their heads. They sat with him on the ground seven days and seven nights, and no one spoke a word to him, for they saw that his suffering was very great.

We don't know how old Job's three friends were, but they must have been older men, since when Elihu appears on the scene he alludes to the fact that they *were* older. Everyone seems to be hard on Job's friends, who seemed so pre-occupied with proving their theology was right that they didn't reach Job's pain.

They told Job that God was just, making bad things happen to bad people and good things happen to good people. They said that this being the case, Job must have done something bad to merit the calamities that had come to him. Job later exclaimed, 'You are worthless physicians, all of you! If only you would be altogether silent! For you, that would be wisdom' (Job 13:4–5, NIV).

We are so quick to condemn Job's friends for not helping Job with his problem that we forget they sat with him in silence for seven long days and nights. Campbell Morgan wrote, 'For seven days they sat with him in silence. That is of the very essence of friendship... They never spoke until he did. All they said was in answer to his first outpouring of grief made possible by their sublime and sympathetic silence.'[13]

It is sad that Job's friends turned from comforters to accusers. If only they had continued to sit in silence with Job, but they had to convince him of their theology. But Job's friends do point the way to help people in pain. So often we think we have to say the right word when people suffer. So we mouth such platitudes as 'I know just how you feel', or 'You are doing so well', or 'It is God's will', or 'Others have gone through this as well'.

Our non-anxious presence is what is needed. We need to hold out a hand in the time of loneliness and fear, and sit in silence through the long hours of suffering. Not words, but a silent presence is enough.

PRAYER
Visit a friend who is in trouble. Sit with her or him and make your silence a prayer.

51

JOB 28:12–28

WHERE IS WISDOM TO BE FOUND?

But where shall wisdom be found? And where is the place of understanding? ... Then [God] saw it and declared it; he established it, and searched it out. And he said to humankind, 'Truly the fear of the Lord, that is wisdom; and to depart from evil is understanding.'

Hanging on my study wall is a well-known picture of an aged man saying grace. His gnarled hands are folded in prayer over a piece of bread and a glass of water. His old face is filled with a quiet splendour that speaks of a wisdom beyond our understanding.

Job says that we may discover all that is hidden except one thing—wisdom. He describes the process by which metals and precious stones are mined: 'the thing that is hid [man] brings forth to light' (28:11)

But wisdom is not something you can either find by searching, or purchase, nor is it something that comes automatically with age. (We all know people who are old but not wise.) Yet, although young people may be wise among their own peer group, it is impossible for them to have the kind and degree of wisdom that older people have acquired. Wisdom is a quality in human beings that is gained through life experiences. It is a process by which a person acts wisely because of the insights that life has given her or him. Yet wisdom is not necessarily associated with the old, but rather is a gift of God bestowed at any age and to whomever he chooses.

Job says that wisdom comes from reverence of God. 'The fear of the Lord, that is wisdom' (28:28). Older persons who have wisdom don't have to *do* anything. We recognize them and cherish them. We affirm the way they know their limitations, focus on what's important and avoid the trivial. Furthermore, as the Talmud says, 'Everyone whose deeds are more than his wisdom, his wisdom endures. And everyone whose wisdom is more than his deeds, his wisdom does not endure. Truly wise older people prove their wisdom by their deeds.'

When 'the shadows lengthen across this little landscape of life', as the old hymn puts it, richness and beauty and depth can be found in those who are like the old man, praying over his bread and water.

PRAYER

O God, we pray you will give us that wisdom which your servant James described as 'pure, then peaceable, gentle, willing to yield, full of mercy and good fruits, without a trace of partiality or hypocrisy' (James 3:17).

52

JOB 42:7–17

WHEN INTEGRITY IS REWARDED

And the Lord restored the fortunes of Job when he had prayed for his friends; and the Lord gave Job twice as much as he had before… The Lord blessed the latter days of Job more than his beginning… After this Job lived one hundred and forty years, and saw his children, and his children's children, four generations. And Job died, old and full of days.

The ending of the story of Job always baffled me. The story of how he kept his integrity when his righteousness was not rewarded is rich in meaning. Job proved that we can love God not for what we get out of it but simply because it is the right thing to do. I always cherished the message out of the whirlwind, when Job repented and said to God, 'I had heard of you by the hearing of the ear, but now my eye sees you' (Job 42:5). Job didn't get answers to his questions; he got God, and that was his answer.

The last chapter seems totally out of place, out of step with the story. Job's riches are not only restored but doubled, and even his children are replaced. This 'happily-ever-after' ending seems to undercut the message of the book.

Life simply doesn't always turn out that way, especially for older people. Losses are not regained; health does not return and often troubles multiply. In some of his earlier words, Job must have had older people in mind, 'Human beings are born to trouble, just as sparks fly upward' (Job 5:7). But, Job's protest against the popular doctrine of that time—if you obey, you are blessed; if you sin, you suffer—now seems like idle words. After all, being righteous pays off in the end, doesn't it?

Some interpreters believe that the epilogue was tacked on at the end of the book by someone who had to show that goodness does bring rewards in this life. But theologian Carol M. Bechtel helped me see this epilogue in a new light. She believes it took far more courage for Job to 'be' than 'not to be'.[14] For Job to reinvest in family and community life, after experiencing such devastating losses, took real faith.

Older people who suffer devastating losses in later life need the tenacious faith that Job portrays. It takes a lot of courage and grit to live again when we know what it means to be near death. It takes a lot more trust to love again when we know what it means to lose that love.

PRAYER

Lord, help me begin again, when I would rather not.

53

PSALM 6

WHEN LIFE TUMBLES IN

Be gracious to me, O Lord, for I am languishing; O Lord, heal me, for my bones are shaking with terror. My soul also is struck with terror, while you, O Lord—how long? … The Lord has heard my supplication; the Lord accepts my prayer.

A few years ago, after my retirement, I suffered serious complications from surgery. I returned home like a wounded old dog who had suffered a resounding defeat at the hands of a younger foe and crawled home to lick his wounds. Never in my life had I felt such weakness and utter dismay.

My sickness and long days and nights of recovery hurled me into a 'dark night of the soul', that agonizing time when one seeks contact with God and finds only empty isolation. My anguish made me bombard the heavens with questions that had no answers. I had just settled down to enjoy a well-deserved retirement, and it seemed as if I would never recover.

One interminable autumn day, I began to wonder if I would ever get well, and I fantasized that I would spend my final days like this—confined at home, unable to drive, dependent on others for bare necessities, staring out of the window at a world that had suddenly come to a screeching halt. Becoming an old, disabled man no longer seemed a future possibility; it had become a present reality.

What helped turn me around were the Psalms, which emerged out of others' experiences of being overwhelmed, nearly destroyed, and which, surprisingly, gave me life and hope. There is no cover-up of feelings in the Psalms. I felt that the words of Psalm 6 were written for me.

The person in the psalm was seriously ill. Physical vigour was waning, body and life were disturbed, groaning and grief filled all his days, and death was an imminent possibility. My own pain, anger and dismay that life is not always good was mirrored in this psalm.

But in verse 8, the tone changed and the psalmist gave thanks that his prayer for health had been granted. In time I found healing from my sickness, but those agonizing moments when life came to the edge of the precipice will always be a part of me. We never forget the times when life gets out of focus. Like the psalmist, I crawled out of the belly of my despair to be given a second chance... by the grace of God.

REFLECTION

We give thanks, O God, for all times when life tumbled in, and we were given a new beginning.

54

PSALM 23

THE LIFE REVIEW OF AN OLD SHEPHERD

The Lord is my shepherd, I shall not want... Surely goodness and mercy shall follow me all the days of my life, and I shall dwell in the house of the Lord my whole life long.

The 23rd Psalm is the best-known and best-loved passage in the Bible. It is divinely simple, and simply divine. Invariably, older people find themselves coming back again and again to these words for comfort and strength. It was only recently that I saw this psalm in a new light.

In an old trunk, I unearthed a musty book, an exposition of the 23rd Psalm by my uncle, Dr F. Crossley Morgan. He writes:

Evidently at the time of writing, David, the old shepherd, was in a reminiscent mood. He was recalling his life as a shepherd, remembering the many things he had done for the sheep; then in the midst of his reminiscing there came a moment of illumination, a moment when in effect he said to himself, 'Everything I did once for the sheep, God has been doing for me all along the pathway of life!'[15]

David remembered how he made the sheep lie down in green pastures and led them beside still waters, into the right paths. He recalled protecting the sheep with rod and staff in dark valleys, and providing healing and hospitality in the desert. On a much deeper level, Yahweh the Shepherd had provided rest, guidance, a loving presence and sanctuary for the old shepherd.

A famous actor returned to his home town to be honoured for his achievements in drama. Sitting in the audience was his old pastor, now retired. Someone reminded the actor that he had recited the 23rd Psalm as a boy in Sunday school, and asked if he would recite it again. He agreed, if his old pastor would do likewise. After the actor had recited the psalm, the audience applauded, moved by his eloquence. The old minister stumbled over the words, but when he sat down the silence of eternity flooded the room. The actor turned to his host and whispered, 'I know the 23rd Psalm, but my old pastor knows the shepherd.'

PRAYER

Loving Shepherd, even as old sheep we often stray from your way and carelessly pursue our own ends, yet we know that your love restores our souls.

55

Psalm 37

THE MERRY-GO-ROUND OF LIFE

Do not fret because of the wicked; do not be envious of wrongdoers, for they will soon fade like the grass, and wither like the green herb… I have been young, and now am old, yet I have not seen the righteous forsaken or their children begging bread. They are ever giving liberally and lending, and their children become a blessing.

Another psalm that David wrote in his later years shows how life can be a merry-go-round of ups and downs. Psalm 37 deals with some of the raw edges of life, when it becomes hard to keep the faith. David had such moments, when it appeared that evildoers were in control. Yet, in his mature wisdom, he could say, 'I have been young, and now am old, yet I have not seen the righteous forsaken.'

Growing older, I realize that life is not like the races I used to run in college, but more like the rides I so loved on the beachfront merry-go-round. I can still remember those merry-go-round rides, whirling around and around amid the flashing lights and happy music, on those horses that leaped up and down. The world beyond the merry-go-round seemed to fade away, and the reality became the merry-go-round and the people who shared this whirling world with me.

Now, however, when I take my grandchildren on the merry-go-round, I usually sit with old folks in those gaily decorated carriages sprinkled here and there among the leaping horses. My days for riding the horses have ended, but the happy music and flashing lights are as good as ever.

The 37th Psalm makes us aware that the life of the spirit is a merry-go-round. There are difficulties and dangers as we ride up and down in our faith journeys. Yet always, God is present if we commit our way to him.

As a child, when I rode the merry-go-round, I always kept my eye on my father, who stood a few feet from my twirling life, ready to take me home when the ride ended. So, God the Father stands at our sides throughout the experiences of this life. Our topsy-turvy worlds are always encircled by the infinite, eternal Father, who stands but a few feet away. We know, too, that at any moment our ride could end and the Father will reach out, take our hand, help us down and take us home with him.

REFLECT ON THESE WORDS
Trust in the Lord. Commit your way to the Lord.

56

PSALM 42 (NIV)

GROWING OLDER, GETTING DEPRESSED

Why are you downcast, O my soul? Why so disturbed within me?
Put your hope in God, for I will yet praise him, my Saviour and
my God. My soul is downcast within me… Deep calls to deep in
the roar of your waterfalls; all your waves and breakers have
swept over me.

She is a widow, 80 years old, who lives alone. Her health is
beginning to fail and she worries about the future. Where will
she go when she can no longer manage at home? She dare not
let her children know about her anxieties, lest they whisk
her off to a nursing home. So she spends her days being
depressed.

He had been a powerful executive of a large company, but
now he just can't seem to shake the blues. 'I take pills to get
through the day and sedatives at night to sleep. My energy is
gone, and it is not possible to find any joy in life,' he told me.
He stays depressed all the time.

Over 25 percent of older people suffer from depression,
but often it is undiagnosed and untreated, so they suffer in

silence. It seems to steal over anyone as insidiously as a London fog, chilling the heart and sapping the energy. For older people, it can be a nightmare in slow motion. Older people are particularly vulnerable to depression. Loss of health, confinement to smaller space, the endless monotony of time, loss of friends and spouses and awareness of death all play a role.

We must beware of the glib clichés and quick fixes. We must avoid saying, 'We all have bad days', or 'You'll pull out of it', or 'Just have faith'. Some people may recall Felix Powell's song of optimism, 'Pack up your troubles in your old kit bag, and smile, smile, smile.' It sustained morale for millions of Britons through two World Wars. But Powell committed suicide!

The 42nd Psalm has a familiar ring to older people. The psalmist knew depression. He spoke about being 'downcast in soul', now that he was cut off from the worshipping community. He remembered the thundering cataracts that pour down in springtime from the melting snows of Mount Hermon, and their roar and echo, and he used that memory to describe his experience: 'deep calls to deep at the roar of your waterfalls'. The shallows could not suffice, only the depths. So he cried, 'Put your hope in God, for I will yet praise him, my Saviour and my God.' There is hope in God.

PRAYER

When life closes in, when our days are long and difficult, help us, O God, not to despair.

57

The prayer of an old man

Do not cast me off in the time of old age; do not forsake me when my strength is spent... O God, do not be far from me. O my God, make haste to help me! ... So even to old age and gray hairs, O God, do not forsake me, until I proclaim your might to all the generations to come.

This is one time in the Bible where we know the prayer is made by an old person. The writer makes it clear that he is an older person, and not a youth, since the psalm in some places is so exuberant, one could mistake the psalmist for a younger person.

Psalm 71 seems to be the desperate yet confident prayer of an older person—desperate because his enemies are treating him shamefully; confident because the God of his youth still listens. He knows full well that in his society people take advantage of the old, and prey on the aged. He lives on the edge of society, with rights denied.

The psalmist looks back at his life and recognizes the care of God from his birth and through all the trials of his life. He feels confident that this same God will not forsake him when he is old and grey-headed. His one hope is to turn to God who protects the defenceless.

Ronald Blythe, commenting on ageing in the United Kingdom, points out:

The old have been made to feel that they have been sentenced to life and turned into a matter of public concern. They are the first generation of full-timers, and thus, the first generations of old people for whom the state, experimentally, grudgingly, and uncertainly, is having to make special supportive conditions.[16]

The psalmist also wants to declare God's strength to this generation and God's power to all in the future. His prayer is that the faith that has sustained him through all the trials of his life might become a legacy for future generations—'until I proclaim your might to all the generations to come'.

The 71st Psalm becomes a modern prayer for old people who are often denied justice in a youth-obsessed society. In turning to God for support, the psalmist highlights his expectation of others, that all persons should act with dignity, respect and honour for the aged.

REFLECTION

If you are an old person today, write a prayer that expresses your needs and desires.

58

PSALM 88

THE ALZHEIMER SUFFERER'S PSALM

O Lord, God of my salvation, when, at night, I cry out in your presence, let my prayer come before you; incline your ear to my cry. For my soul is full of troubles, and my life draws near to Sheol. I am counted among those who go down to the Pit; I am like those who have no help, like those forsaken among the dead, like the slain who lie in the grave, like those whom you remember no more.

In 1981, Lewis Thomas dubbed Alzheimer's disease 'the disease of the century', while others call it 'the ageing brain's most heartbreaking disorder'. We have all watched friends or loved ones go through the stages of this disease, from forgetfulness to confusion and finally dementia. It becomes the funeral that never ends. Care-givers face years of 36-hour days with little help available.

The 88th Psalm is an individual lament of a person with an extended period of serious illness during which the writer was forced by the slow ebb of his physical powers to realize the loss of his relationship with God, the loss of his very being. His illness is a return to non-existence, which is death. The psalm closes with a despairing cry: 'You have caused friend and neighbour to shun me; my companions are in darkness' (v. 18). How clearly this describes the experience of those with Alzheimer's.

Slow physical deterioration and weakened social relationships have profound spiritual significance, for they can separate a person from God. The experience of the writer of Psalm 88, whose sickness leads to a relentless progression towards death, is mirrored in a person with Alzheimer's disease, for it produces chaos in the part of our body that is most central to our imaging of God in this life. When our minds are destroyed, we lose touch with reality, and all we know are our immediate demands. The God of our salvation must seem distant indeed.

We must never forget that the person with Alzheimer's is a child of God, that all human beings are created in God's own image and are worthy of respect and protection, especially those who cannot care for themselves or who do not measure up to the world's standards of value. God never forgets even the least of his children.

PRAYER

Loving God, you love us regardless of what happens to us or what we have become. We pray for those afflicted with Alzheimer's disease. In their darkness, may we bring your light.

59

PSALM 90:1–10

FACING OUR MORTALITY

For all our days pass away under your wrath; our years come to an end like a sigh. The days of our life are seventy years, or perhaps eighty, if we are strong; even then their span is only toil and trouble; they are soon gone and we fly away.

In the USA, we were all touched by the amazing story of reporter Mitch Albom, his old college professor, Morrie Schwartz, and their relationship during the last weeks of Morrie's life, chronicled in the best-selling book, *Tuesdays with Morrie* (Random House, 2000). We were reminded of the amazing courage and wisdom of a dying man. For several years, I had the wonderful experience of 'Tuesdays with Harry', a 95-year-old man near the end of his life.

One visit sticks in my memory. Harry was ready to die, and asked me to pray that God would send angels to take him home. He wanted to go to sleep and never wake up. I prayed that prayer for Harry, and he prayed for me. He did 'finish his life like a sigh'. Months after his death, my moments with Harry remain, when he faced mortality and death.

Some believe that the 90th Psalm was written by Moses near the end of his long life. He contrasts the eternity of God with the transience of human life. Whatever else the psalms make us feel, we know the frailty of our tenure among all the things we have come to love. The years slip by quickly and soon life will end. We know full well that we will never have enough time to realize all our dreams and fulfil all our hopes, because the sands in the hourglass do run lower. If the psalmist were writing today, in light of our extended years, he might have written, 'If we are fortunate to reach the ripe old age of ninety, or the unusual age of one hundred, the years are full of toil and trouble.' However long we may live, our time is limited and life is terminal.

David Steele, a Presbyterian minister, wrote some poignant words shortly before his death from cancer. He wrote:

My hope is to live until April 6. On that day I will be 70. As a boy I recall when my grandfather turned 70. He told me, 'Three-score years and ten, that's what the Bible says is a full life.' If I could make that, I'd have no grounds for regret, would I?[17]

REFLECTION
Time, like an ever-rolling stream,
Bears all its sons away;
They fly forgotten, as a dream
Dies at the opening day.
Isaac Watts (1674–1748)

60

MAKING FRIENDS WITH TIME

Who considers the power of your anger? Your wrath is as great as the fear that is due you. So teach us to count our days that we may gain a wise heart. Turn, O Lord! How long? Have compassion on your servants! Satisfy us in the morning with your steadfast love, so that we may rejoice and be glad all our days.

When we realize how little time we may have left to realize our dreams and fulfil our plans, time has become our enemy. When we were younger, we always looked forward to the future. We eagerly anticipated things out there with real excitement. But no longer. We cannot escape the reality that life is approaching its end, and what seemed possible now seems less and less likely to happen in the time left.

How can we once more make friends with time? We may have little control over the quantity of time left to us, but we have considerable control over the quality of time left. The words of the 90th Psalm bring us an answer: 'So teach us to count our days...' (we have done that!) '...that we may gain a wise heart'. What does that mean? We need to stop wasting precious moments griping about the passage of time and get on with realizing that the present moments are full of grace.

We need to get rid of some of the trivial pursuits of our lives and realize the sacredness of each moment. The Bengali poet and philosopher Rabindranath Tagore once wrote, 'The butterfly counts not minutes, but moments, and has time enough.' We need to be awakened to the preciousness of life, living our lives fully and with care for others.

We need to affirm the small things that give time its blessed quality—a touch, a glance, a sound, a tiny ritual. We can realize that the finiteness of our limited moments makes them all the more precious. The psalmist prays that 'we may gain a wise heart', meaning that we drink deeply of every moment and cherish whatever time we have left.

The apostle Paul calls us to 'redeem the time' (Ephesians 5:16, NKJV), which means not frittering away our time in meaningless things but filling it with vital involvement, creative play, family relationships and time for God.

REFLECTION
Someone has said that we have two lives to live, one here and one after death. Tomorrow, or the next life—you never know which will come first.

61

PSALM 92

GROWING OLD WITH DIGNITY

The righteous flourish like the palm tree, and grow like a cedar in Lebanon. They are planted in the house of the Lord; they flourish in the courts of our God. In old age they still produce fruit; they are always green and full of sap.

Some people believe that life has a peak somewhere, with an upward and downward slope on either side. The peak is flanked by valleys, one rising, the other declining. For many people, the peak is mid-life, and from that moment on it is always downhill.

But the psalmist says that we need to be fresh and flourishing in our old age. He was probably thinking of the cedar of Lebanon—tall, beautiful and long-lived. Service, vitality and productivity are not to end as long as we live. Life is peaks and valleys throughout the journey, and even in old age we can be fruitful.

Sometimes those words haunt us as we confront the inevitable issues of older age. Our trees have grown older and the gnarled limbs, scarred trunks and dry leaves bear witness to what time has done to us. How can we bear fruit, be green and flourishing, still filled with life's juice and sap?

We bring to old age the person we have been all our lives. All that we have been in the earlier years matures and flowers in old age.

Author Velma Wallis tells the story of two elderly women from a Native American migrating tribe in Alaska who were abandoned by the tribe when they faced starvation brought on by the harsh Arctic weather and a shortage of game and fish. The two women, branded old and useless by the tribe, discerned ways to survive their fate, and even found food to share with the tribe. The tribe appointed these women to honorary positions, and promised never again to abandon their elders. These old 'trees' continued to flourish and keep the faith, not only surviving the sentence of their own death but bringing new hope to all the elderly of the Gwich'in people who lived on the upper Yukon River in Alaska.

All of us want to die with dignity. But we should also pray that we may live out our final days with dignity.

PRAYER

Understanding God, you know our weakness and limitations. We are graven on the palm of your hand. But give us strength to be fresh and green as long as we live on this earth.

62

PSALM 137:1–6 (NIV)

WHEN LIFE IS LIVED IN
THE MEANTIME

*By the rivers of Babylon we sat and wept when we remembered
Zion. There on the poplars we hung our harps, for there our
captors asked us for songs, our tormentors demanded songs of
joy; they said, 'Sing us one of the songs of Zion!' How can we
sing the songs of the Lord while in a foreign land? If I forget you,
O Jerusalem, may my right hand forget its skill.*

It was sad as I watched a garage sale at an old friend's home—
fragments of her life merchandized from racks and tables,
gone in casual dismissal. A lifetime of living and homemaking
stacked and bagged and sold for peanuts (nothing over a
dollar). Her first and only home gone on the auction block
while she was shuffled off to a nursing home. She went
silently but with that look on her face of sheer terror, as the
old had passed away and she faced an unknown future.

Life is lived in the meantime. Those ancient Hebrew
captives were miles from their home, staring at a strange land,
filled with homesickness that seemed like an eternity. When
the cruel captors asked them to sing a hymn of praise, they

cried, 'How can we sing the songs of the Lord in a strange land?' Surely not here, in Babylon!

No longer were they in the place where they had raised their children, worshipped in the temple, built a lifetime of memories. They had been taken forcibly from everything that gave life meaning and had become displaced persons with no identity. No wonder they wanted to hang it up and leave their harps on poplar trees.

But from the depths of their despair, arose a cry of faith. 'If I forget you, O Jerusalem…' In that moment when they remembered Jerusalem, faith was rekindled and hope reborn. Instead of sitting paralysed with despair, and moping about how bad things were, they were to lift their hearts to Jerusalem, trusting Yahweh enough once again to sing the songs of Zion.

Being uprooted or displaced in later life is a rude shock and never easy. It is living in the meantime, between a closed past and an uncertain future. Rather than 'hang up our harps', we need to 'hang in there' and keep the faith. A paradigm for this stage in our faith journey is relinquishment (letting go of the past), trust (living by faith in the interim time) and transformation (a new beginning).

PRAYER

Lord of the journey, help me to relinquish the past, live by trust in the present, and believe that your spirit will bring future transformation.

63

PROVERBS 4:1–9, 20–27 (NIV)

WORDS FOR THE NEXT GENERATION

Listen, my sons, to a father's instruction; pay attention and gain understanding… Get wisdom, get understanding; do not forget my words or swerve from them. Do not forsake wisdom, and she will protect you; love her, and she will watch over you. Wisdom is supreme; therefore get wisdom.

At the end of a conference on preparing clergy to minister to the aged, a young Moravian pastor stood and said, 'I have heard a lot of ideas and suggested strategies for ministry with older persons. But the best preparation you can give us is to provide role models of creative ageing.' It is true that ageing remains a mystery to the young. They are ill-equipped to understand their parents, and their grandparents often fade from the scene long before death. So youth grow up without models of graceful ageing.

Although there are only a few references in the book of Proverbs to ageing, the book is full of the wisdom of elders handed down to the next generations. Although the words of Proverbs 4 were meant as a father's legacy to his son, they also typify the wisdom that the older generation needs to leave for the younger generation.

I was once asked on a television interview to offer guidelines on retirement for the younger generation. This is what I said:

- Expand your horizons and do things unlike anything you have done before.
- Do not go along with what the media and the dominant culture are telling you. Decide for yourself what your mission and life values are.
- Be rebellious. Take some risks.
- Find a creative balance between remaining active and finding time for your inner life. Being too busy can be a form of violence against yourself.
- Be a responsible elder by mentoring someone younger than you.

If you are an older person, what wisdom would you offer to the younger generation? The words of Proverbs still ring true, 'Train a child in the way he should go, and when he is old, he will not turn from it' (Proverbs 22:6, NIV). Perhaps in this day of increasing longevity we need to add, 'Give wisdom to those who are in middle age, and when they are old they will not depart from it.'

REFLECTION

What counsel would you offer to a younger person about growing old?

64

PROVERBS 20:1–29 (NIV)

BE PROUD OF YOUR WHITE HAIR

The lamp of the Lord searches the spirit of a man; it searches out his inmost being… The glory of young men is their strength, grey hair the splendour of the old.

We live in an age that exalts youth and attempts to disguise age. There is a growing practice called 'anti-ageing' medicine, which includes aesthetic surgery, restorative dentistry and cosmetic dermatology. Face creams, face lifts and chemical peels are advertised that will slow or even prevent the signs of ageing. Some formulas promise that you will look and feel twenty years younger if you swallow their pills or apply their potions and lotions.

Billboards, radio and television ads and the beautifully persuasive displays in our modern magazines all tend to focus on the worth of youth and the worthlessness of age.

How different are the words of the writer of the Proverbs, who says that grey hair is 'the splendour of the old' and, 'Grey hair is a crown of splendour; it is attained by a righteous life' (Proverbs 16:31). In Israel, the 'elders in the gate' were the symbols of the continuity of the community, and great respect was attached to their age.

In the colonial times of the 18th century, the elderly were the most powerful group in American society. Contemporary fashion placed grey wigs and stooped shoulders even on the young. Census reports indicate that persons reported themselves to be older than they were. As the Puritan Increase Mather said, grey heads were wiser than green ones. But then that changed.

In our society, ageism has a face lift. The new way of valuing older people is to highlight their youthfulness and praise them for looking young and behaving likewise. Ageing has become a social crime. How far we are distanced from biblical times and the respect shown to elders. In the Old Testament we are commanded to rise in respect: 'Rise in the presence of the aged, show respect for the elderly and revere your God' (Leviticus 19:32, NIV). Let us value the signs of ageing—wrinkled, weathered faces, lined by years of lived experience; and yes, even white hair!

AFFIRMATION
Be proud of your white hair. Cherish your wrinkles as service stripes. Accept your arthritic hands as badges of experience.

65

ECCLESIASTES 12:1–8 (NJKV)

WHAT'S SO GOOD ABOUT GETTING OLD?

Remember now your Creator in the days of your youth, before the difficult days come, and the years draw near when you say, 'I have no pleasure in them.' … In the day when the keepers of the house tremble, and the strong men bow down; when the grinders cease because they are few, and those that look through the windows grow dim… And desire fails. For man goes to his eternal home, and the mourners go about the streets.

Some have quipped that King Solomon wrote the Song of Songs in his youth, Proverbs in middle age, and Ecclesiastes when he had turned bitter in old age. Ecclesiastes 12 tells with wide-eyed honesty what happens to old people. Readers are warned to remember their Creator in the days of their youth before the creaky days come. For the writer, the shadow of decline and death hang over the powerful as well as the oppressed.

Like an old house, human beings get run down: strong backs are bent, bright eyes are dim, we begin to be afraid of falling, our hair turns white, we shuffle our feet along, and sex can be such a struggle! Hearing gets duller, the windows of the mind fog up and one's sleep is shallow and easily disturbed. And death, when 'the silver cord is loosed, the golden bowl broken, and the pitcher shattered at the fountain' (v. 6, NKJV), looms ever nearer. Each metaphor is a specific reference to a part of the body that deteriorates in old age. As one older man put it, 'What doesn't hurt doesn't work!'

No longer agile and mobile, such older people have become the creaky old. Every day is a challenge and every night a battle against pain. While we applaud the marvels of modern medicine that make ageing easier, no one can deny the inevitable losses and debilities that will come. So, what's so good about getting old?

Yet, even this pessimistic writer offers a clue. After searching for meaning in many different pursuits, he concludes, 'However many years a man may live, let him enjoy them all. But let him remember the days of darkness, for they will be many. Everything to come is meaningless' (Ecclesiastes 11:8, NIV). But tucked in at the end of this gloomy book is one sentence that brings meaning to one's life: 'Fear God, and keep his commandments; for that is the whole duty of everyone (Ecclesiastes 12:13).

That is what is good about getting old.

PRAYER

Gracious God, when our strength fails and our arms grow weak, help us to reverence you.

66

Isaiah 40:27–31

KNOWING OUR LIMITATIONS

He gives power to the faint, and strengthens the powerless. Even youths will faint and be weary, and the young will fall exhausted; but those who wait for the Lord shall renew their strength, they shall mount up with wings like eagles, they shall run and not be weary, they shall walk and not faint.

Recently I saw a bumper sticker that said, 'If you can't run with the big dogs, then stay on the porch!' At first that irritated me, for, despite my older age, I felt I could still run with the big dogs. On second thought, I realized the wisdom in those words, for the limits that come with age can be a peaceful release. We need to stay out of stressful situations and realize our limits and diminishments.

The prophet of the Exile spoke to a defeated, discouraged nation who longed for return to their home. They knew their limits: 'even youths will faint... and the young will fall exhausted'. Imagine the plight of the elders! 'But those who wait for the Lord shall renew their strength, they shall mount up with wings like eagles.' Here the people of God would be reminded of the first exodus from Egypt, when Yahweh 'bore them on eagles' wings' (Exodus 19:4). A new exodus was in the making, which would exceed their fondest dreams. We need to be realistic about our limits when we grow older. New ventures may be precluded by lack of time and energy. No one expects us now to run a marathon or launch into a new career. We are saved from our restless compulsion to do more, to build empires and launch new projects. Finally, we can wait on the Lord, and rest.

Although we allow others to take the lead, we can still walk and not run. God does call us to be involved when we are older, but in different and quieter ways. Perhaps the prophet meant that 'youth shall run and not be weary, and the elders walk and not faint'. Knowing our limits does not mean that we fade into oblivion and watch the world go by from the porch. Rather, in quiet and meaningful ways we choose the right moment for our involvement. We know that God has begun the process of fitting us with those wings that will carry us to eternity, where we will fly higher and faster than we ever did in this life.

REFLECTION

What are some of the things that limit us as we grow older? How do we face them?

67

THE GOD WHO CARRIES US IN OLD AGE

Bel bows down, Nebo stoops… They stoop, they bow down together; they cannot save the burden, but themselves go into captivity. Listen to me, O house of Jacob… who have been borne by me from your birth, carried from the womb; even to your old age I am he, even when you turn grey I will carry you. I have made, and I will bear; I will carry and will save.

This remains the perennial favourite Old Testament passage for older people. It reminds us that we are not alone, that God carries and and supports us even to 'grey hairs'.

The prophet contrasts two faiths: the Babylonians lug their gods into captivity, and when they cry to them there is no answer. Bel and Nebo, the greatest of the gods of the Babylonian religion, cannot save their country or their people, but must themselves go into captivity. Furthermore, *they* have to carry these gods, loading them on to beasts as they flee from the armies of Cyrus.

By contrast, the God of Israel, who carried Israel from her birth, will continue to carry them into her old age. They don't have to carry or prop up their God. Their God carries them and keeps them on their feet. Whatever the difficulty, however painful the burden, God is able to carry us and see us through. That becomes the difference between a religion that we carry and one that carries us. Simply put, is our faith a weight we carry, or wings that carry us?

Even in old age, religion can be a burden we carry—such as religious rituals that have no meaning or pious performance that never helps. We are called by the prophet to remember a God who carries us, who doesn't need our work or effort but who supports and carries us by his grace.

A woman stayed home for many years caring for her aged parents. Each day as she served a cup of tea, she stared at a picture of the Rock of Gibraltar on the lid of the tea caddy. After her parents died, she took a trip to the Mediterranean Sea, and suddenly, as she looked through the porthole of the ship, she saw the Rock of Gibraltar. She exclaimed, 'Why, it's real. It's been real all the time!' We may not realize it at the time, but looking at the events of our life we can say that God's presence and strength have been real all the time.

PRAYER

Help us to know, O God who carries us, that your loving support and strength have been real all the time.

68

ISAIAH 51:1–8 (NJB)

LOOK TO OUR PARENTS

Listen to me, you who pursue saving justice, you who seek Yahweh. Consider the rock from which you were hewn, the quarry from which you were dug. Consider Abraham your father and Sarah who gave you birth. When I called him he was the only one but I blessed him and made him numerous.

For those who have ageing parents, it is extremely difficult to understand them. Parenthood is always an ever-changing mystery, and there is a tendency for us to underestimate parents when we have outgrown them; they are old now and do not understand us. They live in different worlds from ours, locked in the same old stories they love to tell, endless complaints and worrisome habits that we sometimes can't tolerate.

The prophet urged the people of Israel to remember their spiritual parents, Abraham and Sarah, for they were 'the rock from which they were hewn'. These words were spoken to the people who remained in the waste places of Jerusalem. They would be comforted that promises made to their spiritual parents would not be denied. They needed to take a second look at Abraham and Sarah, their spiritual parents. Abraham, knight of faith, carried to his grave the memory of that moment on Mount Moriah when he almost sacrificed his son, Isaac. In spite of everything, Abraham never stopped believing that God was going to keep his promise about making him the father of a great nation. Sarah, who laughed when the angel said she would bear a son in her old age, must have gone through agonizing pain when Abraham set out to kill that son. Yet she too clung to the hope that the wildest dream she had ever had would still come true.

It is hard to parent your parents, to watch the mother who gave you birth grow old and helpless. It's painful to watch the father who was always your rock of strength become shifting sand, a confused and disorientated old man.

But, we need to look beyond the obvious and see past all the façade of ageing and helplessness. We need to realize that they still do hold our images in their hearts, and love us, and feel our pain in ways we cannot understand. And they still have dreams for us.

PRAYER

Lord, help us to see our older parents in a new light, and realize their love for us.

69

JEREMIAH 18:1–6

THE POTTER'S PURPOSE
FOR OLD CLAY

So I went down to the potter's house, and there he was working at his wheel. The vessel he was making of clay was spoiled in the potter's hand, and he reworked it into another vessel, as seemed good to him. Then the word of the Lord came to me: Can I not do with you, O house of Israel, just as this potter has done? says the Lord. Just like the clay in the potter's hand, so are you in my hand, O house of Israel.

Jeremiah noticed an incredible thing at the potter's house. He saw the potter handle some old clay that had not shaped up the way he intended: with infinite patience and unswerving purpose, the potter reshaped the old clay until it became a beautiful piece of pottery. He could have discarded the marred clay and taken up new clay. But he reworked the old clay.

Jeremiah realized a great truth about Yahweh. When we thwart his purpose and mar his plan, God does not toss us on the junk heap. Rather, God can reshape us and make us after his will.

So often, older people feel they are ignored or forgotten and herded off to pasture. The spectre of retirement means for many that we are useless, worthless and boring. If youth is wasted on the young, then maybe retirement is wasted on the 'old'. The potter still had a purpose for the old clay; and God has a purpose for us, too.

Von Herkomer was a famous sculptor who rose to fame in England. After he had built a studio in London, he brought his aged father to live with him. The old man loved to work with clay. But his hands had become so arthritic, nothing ever seemed to work out right. One night, after looking with dismay at his ruined work, he climbed the stairs to his bedroom, a defeated old man. But his son saw what had happened and stayed up all night, reworking that same old clay until it became a beautiful piece of work. The next morning the old man slowly came down the stairs, and the first rays of the sun fell on his statue. Amazed, he exclaimed, 'I can still do it! It's better than I thought!'

So, God works on the clay of our lives, old though it be, and when we despair and surrender to our fears we can see our lives in the light of God's work, and say, 'It's better than I thought!'

PRAYER

Have Thine own way, Lord,
Have Thine own way.
You are the potter, I am the clay.
Mould me and make me, after Thy will,
While I am waiting, yielded and still.

ADELAIDE A. POLLARD (1862–1934)

70

JEREMIAH 32:1–15

INVESTING IN THE FUTURE

Jeremiah said, 'The word of the Lord came to me: Hanamel son of your uncle Shallum is going to come to you and say, "Buy my field that is at Anathoth, for the right of redemption by purchase is yours." ... Then I took the sealed deed of purchase... and I gave the deed of purchase to Baruch... I charged Baruch, saying, Thus says the Lord of hosts, the God of Israel: Take these deeds... that they may last for a long time. For thus says the Lord of hosts, the God of Israel: Houses and fields and vineyards shall again be bought in this land.'

It seemed a strange, if not insane, purchase of land. The armies of Babylon had Jerusalem under siege, and Jeremiah himself had said that the nation would fall. Such property would be worthless in enemy hands. Babylon would soon occupy the city and own all the land, and Jeremiah's deed would not be worth the paper it was written on.

Jeremiah's purchase of land was no mere investment but a symbol of his faith in God that 'houses and fields and vineyards shall again be bought in this land'. This sacred soil, now scorched by Babylonian armies, would one day return to the Hebrew people. It was his faith in the future, a future he would never see.

Jeremiah's act was a gift for the next generation. He remained in Jerusalem with a group of his fellow citizens under the authority of a ruling governor, appointed by the Babylonians. Later he was forced to seek safety in Egypt and died there. It would be many years before Jeremiah's purchase of land would be redeemed.

An old man, a full 81 years, planted a grove of small pecan trees. Someone asked, 'Why did you not select larger trees, so as to increase the possibility of your living to see them bear at least one cup of nuts? Do you expect to live to see the trees reach sufficient maturity to bear fruit?'

'No,' replied the old man. 'But is that important? All my life I have eaten fruit from trees that I did not plant. Why shouldn't I plant trees to bear fruit for those who may enjoy them long after I am gone?'

A seemingly worthless act—buying land that soon would be in enemy hands, paying good money—such a waste. And yet this act of faith remains a constant witness to all older people, that we too may plant trees. We shall never sit under their shade. But our grandchildren will.

REFLECTION

What may I do or be that will outlive me, and leave a legacy of faith to coming generations?

71

EZEKIEL 22:23–31 (NKJV)

STANDING IN THE GAP

So I sought for a man among them who would make a wall, and stand in the gap before me on behalf of the land, that I should not destroy it; but I found no one.

Throughout the London Underground systems are signs that say 'Mind the gap'. They remind passengers to pay attention to the space between the train and the platform. The words 'Mind the gap' help people to avoid dangerous accidents.

Ezekiel, the temple priest who was carried into captivity into Babylon, ministered to the exiles living near him in Tel-Abib. He lamented the fact that God could not find a man who would 'stand in the gap before me on behalf of the land'. No one stood in the gap.

Ezekiel had stood in the gap between God and the pain of his people. He tells us, 'Then I came to the captives at Tel-Abib, who dwelt by the River Chebar; and I sat where they sat' (Ezekiel 3:15, NKJV). Neither scolding nor scorning these refugees from Jerusalem, Ezekiel identified with their pain and experienced their feelings of desolation and distress.

Gaps present dangers for older people—distances no longer easy to navigate, other problems caused by loss of hearing or vision or mobility. Gaps also exist in relationships—gaps between old friends who drift away, and gaps between family members who can't seem to grasp how older people feel. Sometimes there are even gaps between older people and their churches, which sometimes seem insensitive to their special needs for worship and pastoral care.

Older people need friends who will 'stand in the gap' and be there when needed. Such soul friends listen with gentleness and patience, speak with truth and love, hold out a hand in time of loneliness and fear, sit in silence through the long night watches and rejoice when the shadows flee away as the warm sun brings deliverance. All too often, older people have no one to 'stand in the gap' with them, and they drift into depression or dreary times. But, bless God, there are those care-givers who do 'stand in the gap' and minister to the needs of older people.

PRAYER

Loving God, help me today to 'stand in the gap' and be a soul friend to an older person. May my love for them bring them closer to you. Amen.

72

HOSEA 2:14–23

VALLEYS OF TROUBLE...
THE DOOR OF HOPE

Therefore, I will now allure her, and bring her into the wilderness, and speak tenderly to her. From there I will give her her vineyards, and make the Valley of Achor a door of hope. There she shall respond as in the days of her youth, as at the time when she came out of the land of Egypt.

No one knew better about valleys of trouble than the prophet Hosea. His unhappy family experience with an unfaithful wife, Gomer, caused him pain and rejection. He even named two of his children Lo-Ammi ('not mine') and Lo-Ruhamah ('never knew a father's love'). No doubt he could easily have secured a divorce and forgotten Gomer for ever.

Is there a single life without the Valley of Achor? This valley was so named because Achan brought the 'accursed thing' into the camp and caused the Israelite defeat at Ai (Joshua 7). Older people have their 'Valleys of Achor'. They know full well the sting of failure, defeat and the fainting heart. Some even mourn old sins.

Yet Hosea says that each Valley of Achor has a door of hope.

It was so for Hosea. When he was tempted to give up Gomer, he realized he loved her unconditionally. He could not give her up or turn her over to a life of prostitution.

So this prophet realized the incredible unconditional love of God, who could easily have turned his back on Israel and banished them from his memory. Hosea learned about a God who says, 'How can I give you up, Ephraim? ... I will not execute my fierce anger... for I am God, and no mortal' (Hosea 11:8a, 9).

What Hosea felt for his wayward wife on a human level, the God of Israel felt for his people on a deeper level. So, even in the valley of trouble and sin, there is a door of hope. Out of such experiences Israel would respond as in the days of the exodus. Though the summer is gone, there will be a second—an Indian summer, even better than the first—as God gives you a greater revelation of his love.

Is it any wonder that when the self-righteous religious leaders confronted Jesus with his acceptance of outcasts and street people, he pointed them to the Hosea story and said, 'Go and learn what this means' (Matthew 9:13). Jesus himself opens the door of hope for our valleys of trouble.

REFLECTION
Go and learn what Hosea means—now.

73

Amos 5:14–27

Empowering older people

Seek good and not evil, that you may live; and so the Lord, the God of hosts, will be with you, just as you have said. Hate evil and love good, and establish justice in the gate… But let justice roll down like waters, and righteousness like an everflowing stream.

An elder in the UK who had reached 90 years of age recently told me, 'Older folk today make up what might be called the "far-too-silent" generation. Seldom have we stood up for our rights which were earned over a lifetime of working and sharing, nor have we been critics of a society in which others suffer from inequality and lack of opportunity. We have been silent spectators of what is going on around us.'

I wonder what the prophet Amos would say today regarding injustices inflicted on older people. Amos, the herdsman from Tekoa, was no silent spectator of the social sins and injustices he found in the northern kingdom.

After a roll call of all the sins of the nations around Israel, Amos denounced the sins of a nation that cheated the poor through oppressive taxes (Amos 5:11), sanctioned the wide disparity between the rich and the poor, and sold 'the righteous for silver and the needy for a pair of sandals' (Amos 2:6).

Even the temple priest, Amaziah, could not squelch him or silence his message. Fearlessly, Amos cried out that religion is more than performance, and must be translated into social justice: 'Let justice roll down like waters, and righteousness like an everflowing stream.'

Older people need that kind of prophetic advocate today, as we still live in a society where politicians and pundits toss around the basic, general needs of older people. Perhaps those of a younger generation, when they are ageing, will not be so passive. More educated and worldly-wise, they will become agents of change.

Older people need advocates who will stand up for their rights and make their needs a primary concern. Amos seems a lonely figure on the scene of biblical history. His words were not heeded, nor his cry for justice answered. As the world today experiences the 'age wave', we have time to make changes now that will better the lives of older people.

PRAYER

For prophets who stood for justice and who did not pander to the powerful or kiss the hands of the rich, we thank you, Lord. May there be such prophets today who are advocates for the ageing.

74

HABAKKUK 2:1–4 (NIV)

LORD, GIVE ME PATIENCE NOW

I will stand at my watch and station myself on the ramparts;
I will look to see what he will say to me, and what answer I am
to give to this complaint. Then the Lord replied, 'Write down the
revelation and make it plain on tablets so that a herald may run
with it. For the revelation awaits an appointed time; it speaks of
the end and will not prove false. Though it linger, wait for it; it
will certainly come and will not delay.'

The older I get, the more impatient I become. I had hoped, as I entered my 72nd year, that I would be more patient. But the reverse is true. I am becoming more impatient. My patience wears thin when I have to mark time waiting in the doctor's surgery or fretting at the delay of needed cheques, or when my computer is down. We live in a fast-lane society that demands instant satisfaction, from microwaved meals to instant replays. How many times have I prayed, 'Lord, give me patience *now*!'

The prophet Habakkuk had to learn patience as he sought answers from the Lord. How could God allow such evil to exist in the world? And then, when he discovered that God was using the wicked Babylonians as an instrument of his justice, he became even more agitated. But he learned to wait: 'though it linger, wait for it'. Only later did he get his answer that the evil nation Babylon would fall, and 'the righteous shall live by their faith'.

Like Habakkuk, we too must learn that patience is necessary in the life of the spirit. Older people whose bodies become dry and brittle, like a leaf at year's end, and whose minds at times are not as sharp as in younger years, need patience. Some older people who find that the tag-end of life brings indignities and helplessness, and who yearn for the 'better country', know that being sentenced to life can be as dreadful as being sentenced to death. They need patience— waiting for the end.

In the Gospel of Luke, Christ says, 'In your patience possess your souls' (Luke 21:19, NJKV). So, those of us who are older need to cultivate this virtue and find that rest for the soul. As Francis de Sales wrote, 'Have patience with all things, but chiefly have patience with yourself.' So I will try to be patient with my impatience, and work on it.

PRAYER

Lord, I do try to be patient with others, myself and life, but growing older makes me so impatient with trifling things. Teach me your patience.

75

HAGGAI 2:1–9

THE CURSE OF 'OLD TIMERS'

The word of the Lord came by the prophet Haggai, saying: Speak now to Zerubbabel son of Shealtiel, governor of Judah, and to Joshua son of Jehozadak, the high priest, and to the remnant of the people, and say, Who is left among you that saw this house in its former glory? How does it look to you now? Is it not in your sight as nothing? … The latter splendour of this house shall be greater than the former, says the Lord of hosts; and in this place I will give prosperity.

Progress on rebuilding the temple in Jerusalem had been slow. Either because of constant opposition or discouragement, the Israelites dwelt in panelled houses while the temple remained in ruins. Haggai spoke to the people on the last day of the feast of Tabernacles, probably to those gathered in Jerusalem for the holiday period. His message was mainly directed to some of the old-timers who could recall the former temple of Solomon and felt that any other temple could never compare with it.

Some work had been accomplished, but apparently some of the old-timers were throwing a wet blanket over the present building project. Showing contempt for the building of the new temple and attachment to the old, they felt that any building would pale in comparison to Solomon's temple. These old-timers had a real 'edifice complex' and, like many older people who bolster up their image of the past by exaggerating their accomplishments and magnifying their importance, these old men could not move into a new future.

Although some older people are creative and willing to change, there are always older persons who resist change, hold on to power tight-fistedly and live in the past. These days, there is much talk about young people who refuse to conform to society's norms and are called 'drop-outs'. Old persons who refuse to live in the present and escape into the land of memories also might be called 'drop-outs'.

Haggai had to overcome the resistance of these old-timers by helping the Israelites to realize that the glory of God's new temple would be even greater than the old temple. Elders like Haggai are needed, who recognize that traditions must constantly evolve, in order to avoid stagnation and the excessive veneration of the past that destroys creativity and growth.

PRAYER

O thou that changest not, abide with us, but give us the courage to surrender what is past and move with courage into new ventures.

76

ZECHARIAH 8:1–8 (NJB)

A CURE FOR THE GENERATION GAP

Yahweh says this: I am coming back to Zion and shall live in the heart of Jerusalem. Jerusalem will be called Faithful City and the mountain of Yahweh Sabaoth, the Holy Mountain. Yahweh Sabaoth says this: Aged men and women will once again sit in the squares of Jerusalem, each with a stick to lean on because of their great age. And the squares of the city will be full of boys and girls playing there.

Picture this scene, either in New York's Central Park or London's Hyde Park, or even in Jerusalem today. Here are old folk sitting in the sun, propped up by their canes, while boys and girls race around playing together. Notice that the children are playing safely in the streets of the city. This is the vision Zechariah had of the restored Jerusalem where generations would live together in safety and joy.

Age segregation is a major issue in any society. We learn from early years to spend most of our time with persons whose situations are very much like our own: children with children in schools; adults with adults in the workplace, and older people with older people in day centres or sheltered housing. In many cases, activities that once pulled generations together—caring for frail elders, minding small children, telling family stories—are either ignored or delegated to government-funded service providers.

Is it any wonder that caricatures and wrong impressions exist between generations? Young people let societal images monopolize their approach to those who are old, perceiving us as set in our ways, crotchety, grumpy old people. Older people judge young people by the media, letting student unrest, and stories of violence and drugs in schools and colleges, cast young people in a bad light. In his book *Age Power* (Putnam, 1999), Ken Dychtwald asks whether intergenerational relations will be either 'Melting Pot' or 'Gerassic Park'. The vision of Zechariah paints a different tale. Older people sit in the city squares while children play in the streets. Here is no 'age war' in which generations battle with one another over scarce resources. Older people can be models and mentors, with their wisdom and experience, while young people can offer a refreshing sense of exuberance and energy.

REFLECTION

What are some ways you as an older person can mentor a younger person? What stories would you tell? What values would you commend? What might you learn from a young person?

77

1 MACCABEES 2:15–28 (NJB)

MATTATHIAS WAS A LATE BLOOMER

The king's commissioners then addressed Mattathias as follows, 'You are a respected leader, a great man in this town… Be the first to step forward and conform to the king's decree.' … Raising his voice, Mattathias retorted, 'Even if every nation living in the king's dominion obeys him, each forsaking its ancestral religion to conform to his decrees, I, my sons and my brothers will still follow the covenant of our ancestors. May Heaven preserve us from forsaking the Law.'

One of the most stirring stories in biblical times is that of the revolt of the Maccabees against the attempt of the Hellenistic Jews to forsake the Law and the temple. The revolt began in the village of Modein where the aged Mattathias was a respected leader. Mattathias refused to conform to the demand that they forsake the Law, killed the king's commissioner who was sent to enforce the sacrifice, and rode through the town shouting, 'Let everyone who has any zeal for the Law and takes his stand on the covenant come out and follow me' (1 Maccabees 2:27, NJB).

We know little of this old leader until this moment in Jewish history. He was a good example of a late bloomer, who appeared at a crucial moment in history and became God's man of the hour.

Some time ago, I spotted an unusual tree on a college campus. During the spring, all the other trees would bud and bring forth flowers and leaves, but this particular tree always had a late start in blooming. Some questioned whether the tree should be cut down and discarded, but others said it was a late bloomer.

Thank God for late bloomers. Sir Winston Churchill was in his late 60s and early 70s when he rallied the British against Hitler. He wrote *A History of the English Speaking People* at the age of 82. Johann Wolfgang von Goethe, whose greatest masterpiece, *Faust*, was completed when he was 81, wrote, 'Under this white hair is a volcano!' At the age of 81, Pope John XXIII led the Second Vatican Council, which modernized Roman Catholic liturgy and fostered a spirit of ecumenism with all religious faiths. John Wesley, founder of the Methodist Church, disciplined servant of God, wrote in his journal, aged 87, 'I must do a little for God, before I drop in the dust.' Like the aged priest, Mattathias, all were late bloomers who made significant contributions to the world in their later years.

PRAYER

O God, the Rock of Ages, we praise you for all men and women whose deeds show us that boundaries are limitless for achievement at any age.

78

WISDOM OF SOLOMON 4:7–14 (NJB)

LONG LIFE IS NOT ENOUGH

The upright, though he die before his time, will find rest. Length of days is not what makes age honourable, nor number of years the true measure of life; understanding, this is grey hairs, untarnished life, this is ripe old age.

John was 90 years old as he stood in a Methodist pulpit and told the congregation that we all have two lives to live—one here, and one after death. He said that we all have a birth date and a death date, but what we do along the dash (–) between these two dates makes all the difference. He was a living example of a man whose untarnished life and understanding made him a sage to all.

The writer of the Wisdom of Solomon is very much aware of the fact that common sense, clear thinking and enlightenment come at different ages for different people. Grey hairs and an untarnished life are a goal of ripe old age, but do not come automatically with the passage of years. The writer knew that most Jews felt that long life was the reward for the righteous. We live in a society today where medical science has granted us bonus years. Most people will outlive their parents and grandparents, as we have outlived our expected lifespan. We are preoccupied with living longer, but often we forget about living fully. The ancient writer believed that maturity could also be attained by those much younger. Some older people never surrender their childish ways of thinking; others, much younger, move beyond those youthful ways and show a wisdom and maturity usually seen in later years.

This is indeed wisdom, for as we turn to the pages of the New Testament we find too many elders who resisted change and turned against the young prophet of Nazareth. Jesus himself is *the* example of these words from long ago. He did not have a number of days or length of years. But his was *the* untarnished life, and the wisdom of his words and his saving deeds lives on. His life reminds us that life is not measured by the duration of years but by the donation we make to the world.

REFLECTION

These words were written on the grave of a Christian: 'He worked as if he would live for ever. He lived as if he would die tomorrow.' What do these words mean?

79

MATTHEW 1:1–17

GENEALOGIES DO MATTER

An account of the genealogy of Jesus the Messiah, the son of David, the son of Abraham... So all the generations from Abraham to David are fourteen generations; and from David to the deportation to Babylon, fourteen generations; and from the deportation to Babylon to the Messiah, fourteen generations.

Across the world, searching for family stories and tracing one's heritage is riding a big wave of popularity. Millions of people are 'shaking the family tree' and searching for their ancestors. We are finally realizing that there is no greater treasure than that of an old family Bible which records births, marriages and deaths of family members.

It is fitting that the New Testament begins with the genealogy of Jesus in the first chapter of Matthew. Matthew's genealogy is divided into three segments of fourteen generations each. The significance of these three sets of doubled sevens symbolized the doubly perfect tri-unified line of the Messiah. Along with the 42 fathers, four women are mentioned. Tamar, found to be pregnant long after her husband's death; Rahab, a prostitute; Bathsheba, wife of Uriah, pregnant not by her husband but by King David; and

Ruth, an outsider. Their inclusion reminds us that Jesus' long line of ancestors was not always a line of moral saints but of forgiven sinners. There are black sheep and kissing cousins in every family.

An elderly woman was once asked why she did not skip over the first nine chapters of Chronicles (full of genealogies) but read them all. She replied, 'I would feel dreadful if I got to heaven and met these people and didn't know their names.' Genealogies in the Bible help us to think about the role of real people in the story of redemption.

So doing genealogy is important, for our family histories in every generation unite us far more than shared chromosomes. All of us have invisible imprints from previous generations, and our grandchildren need to know their ancestors and the seminal events that shaped their lives. To know our roots is to have our identities intact. To know our ancestors is to know from whom we have come. Matthew's genealogy not only helps us to realize Jesus' ancestry, but we rejoice that, by faith, we too belong to his family by adoption. 'Who is my mother, and who are my brothers?' (Matthew 12:48). All disciples are part of Jesus' family.

REFLECTION

Lord Jesus Christ, we may joyfully trace our roots back in our own family, but our greatest joy is knowing that we belong to your family.

80

MATTHEW 1:18–25

JOSEPH: UNWORRIED OLD PRESENCE

Now the birth of Jesus the Messiah took place in this way. When his mother Mary had been engaged to Joseph, but before they lived together, she was found to be with child from the Holy Spirit. Her husband Joseph, being a righteous man and unwilling to expose her to public disgrace, planned to dismiss her quietly. But just when he had resolved to do this, an angel of the Lord appeared to him in a dream and said, 'Joseph, son of David, do not be afraid to take Mary as your wife.' … When Joseph awoke from sleep, he did as the angel of the Lord commanded him; he took her as his wife.

Christian tradition has never known quite what to do with Joseph. He vanishes early from the Gospel story (presumably he died), before Jesus is baptized, and is never heard from again. This supports the legend that he was already an old man when he took Mary for his wife. He seems to be a kindly old man in the background, an extra in the drama starring Mary and Jesus.

When he learned that Mary was pregnant out of wedlock, the Law demanded that she be either stoned to death (Deuteronomy 22:21) or put away quietly by a bill of divorce.

Joseph had decided to take the latter course, in order that Mary should not suffer shame or public accusation. When he learned in a dream that the child had been conceived by the Holy Spirit, he believed the dream. If not, he would have gone to the court house to file the divorce papers, and Mary would have been an outcast for ever. So Joseph did the scandalous thing, He married a pregnant fiancée and took her child as his own.

Joseph becomes an older, unworried presence in the Advent story, and in Jesus' early life at Nazareth. It was Joseph who guided Mary to Bethlehem. He stood with Mary as she shivered with new life in a cold stable. It was Joseph who protected Mary from Herod's murderous clutches and who led Mary and the young child to Egypt. It was Joseph who taught the young Jesus his carpenter's trade, and provided the strong support of a fatherly figure. His was a quiet piety, wanting to do the right thing but also not wanting to harm Mary. His faith and commitment made him the guardian of God's only Son.

Joseph the carpenter left us no poetry to sing, no dramatic scenes to depict on Christmas cards, no sensational story for us to recall. But his unworried presence behind the scenes is a role model for all older persons.

PRAYER

Lord, we give thanks for Joseph, an older man whose love and support we should never forget. Help us to be that unworried presence to others.

81

MATTHEW 18:21–35

IT'S NEVER TOO LATE TO FORGIVE

Then Peter came and said to him, 'Lord, if another member of the church sins against me, how often should I forgive? As many as seven times?' Jesus said to him, 'Not seven times, but, I tell you, seventy-seven times.'

Many older people go into their later years carrying grudges and harbouring resentments against family members or friends. This resentment can be called the arthritis of the spirit, for it deforms and cripples our spirits. We use it to protect ourselves, to hurt back before we can be hurt again, but it has a sinister way of circling right back to us so that we are the victims of our own self-will.

We do not know why Peter asked Jesus the question how often he should forgive his brother. He seems to answer his own question in a most generous way, for the Jewish tradition allowed forgiveness up to three times. If Peter's forgiveness stretched to seven times, he was willing to go the extra mile, and then some.

Whether you read Jesus' answer to Peter as 77 times, or 70 times seven, the point is the same. Jesus is making it clear to Peter not to assume that you can count how many times you offer forgiveness and be done with it. Forgiveness is a commitment. It is not a single action, feeling or thought. Peter wanted limits to his forgiveness. Limitless forgiveness is what God demands.

The parable of the unforgiving servant (vv. 23–35) is all too clear. Forgiven a colossal, unpayable debt, he is unwilling to forgive even a small debt owed to him. The debt we owe God is unpayable, and if we truly experience God's limitless grace then we are constrained to show that same forgiveness to everyone who has hurt us.

Older people can be grudge-keepers, holding on to old feelings of resentment and hatred. But forgiveness can release us from the corrosive burden of anger and bitterness that eats away our peace of soul. It can free us from the prison of constantly replaying scenes of old wounds, and even when reconciliation does not occur we are healed and can face each day with clean hearts and new spirits.

PRAYER

'Create in me a clean heart, O God, and put a steadfast spirit within me. Do not cast me away from your presence, and do not take your Holy Spirit from me' (Psalm 51:10–11)

82

MATTHEW 20:1–16

ELEVENTH-HOUR GRACE

And when they received it, they grumbled against the landowner, saying, 'These last worked only one hour, and you have made them equal to us who have borne the burden of the day and the scorching heat.' But he replied to one of them, 'Friend, I am doing you no wrong; did you not agree with me for the usual daily wage? Take what belongs to you and go; I choose to give to this last the same as I give to you.'

It really didn't seem fair! The workmen who had worked only one hour from 5pm until 6pm got the same pay as a workman who had laboured from 6am to 6pm in the gruelling heat of the day. The amazing thing was that no matter how long a workman had worked, he got the same pay. Jesus is saying that God is the householder before whom there is no just wage, for everything we receive comes from his mercy.

The parable also makes it clear that those who come to God at the beginning of their lives are not loved more than those who come at the end of their lives. For some, becoming a Christian happens when the evening shadows fall on their lives. The sinner who repents at the eleventh hour receives the same grace as those who have worked for God all their lives.

No one but God knows who will be first or last in his kingdom, and those who believe they earn it 'by right' strongly risk being among the last.

This parable of eleventh-hour grace has real meaning for older people. It is reassuring to know that the labourers may have worked for different lengths of time but all receive equal pay. God, this parable implies, is always waiting for us to return to him. It makes no difference at what age we begin the journey or how long we struggle. The rewards are equally tremendous for all who answer the call.

Little wonder, then, that the apostle Paul, late in his life, wrote to the Philippians, 'Work out your own salvation with fear and trembling, for it is God who is at work in you' (Philippians 2:12–13). We can never do enough work to earn salvation. We never work *for* it. God's grace has taken care of our salvation in Jesus Christ. But whether we work *out* our salvation through years of struggle or only in our later years, it is always a response to God's inexhaustible grace.

PRAYER
Thank you, God, for eleventh-hour grace, for now in these later years we need that grace. Help us to accept your gift with open hearts.

83

MATTHEW 25:14–30 (NIV)

USE OR LOSE... EVEN IN THE LATER YEARS

But the man who had received the one talent went off, dug a hole in the ground and hid his master's money... Then the man who had received the one talent came. 'Master,' he said, 'I knew that you are a hard man, harvesting where you have not sown and gathering where you have not scattered seed. So I was afraid and went out and hid your talent in the ground. See, here is what belongs to you.' His master replied, 'You wicked, lazy servant! ... You should have put my money on deposit with the bankers, so that when I returned I would have received it back with interest... Take the talent from him.'

As a writer I am always looking for the perfect pen, and on one occasion found just the right gold pen. Since I have a penchant for losing things, I was afraid to use that pen. For months I kept it in a safe place and never used it. One day it dawned on me that this beautiful pen was useless unless I put it to work.

The simple truth of Jesus' parable remains true at any age. If we don't use our talents, we will lose them. The one-talent man did nothing wrong: in fact, he played safe by burying the talent in the ground. Later he admitted he was afraid to take the risk. But, in the end, he lost the talent. It was given to the persons who had used their gifts.

Jesus' parable is as relevant to later life as it is to earlier life, for we are accountable to God all through life for the gifts he has given us. We may not be equal in ability, but every person has the same opportunity to use their talents for God's kingdom. Charles Darwin delighted in poetry and music as a young man. But when he became older, he was so immersed in biology that he had no time to read poetry or listen to music. As an older man, he said he wished he could live his life over, so that poetry and music could have played a greater part.

Older persons may retire from their jobs, but often they have nothing to retire to. Time can become a real problem. Actor George Sanders left a suicide note that read, 'I'm literally bored to death.' Maybe life can be boring in the retirement years if we do not have some purpose, some creative use of our talents. Years ago I saw a sign on a church bulletin board which is relevant to any age: 'What on earth are we doing for Heaven's sake?'

Use or lose! That's the simple equation of the spiritual life.

REFLECTION

Take an inventory of the spiritual gifts that God has given you. How can you use these gifts for the kingdom?

84

MARK 4:1–20 (NIV)

PRESBYCUSIS: AN OLDER PERSON'S PROBLEM

Then Jesus said, 'He who has ears to hear, let him hear... The farmer sows the word. Some people are like seed along the path, where the word is sown. As soon as they hear it, Satan comes and takes away the word that was sown in them. Others, like seed sown on rocky places, hear the word and at once receive it with joy. But since they have no root, they last only a short time.'

A lot of older people don't like to admit that they are losing their hearing—even if they notice it themselves. How many times have we heard older people tell us either 'Speak up' or 'Don't shout at me'. Hearing aids do help, but a lot of older people won't admit they need them.

According to the specialist Mayo Clinic in Minnesota, more than one-third of people over the age of 65 experience some level of hearing loss due to the natural process of ageing. The medical term for this is 'presbycusis'. Hearing loss can affect the quality of life. When you don't hear well, people think you are confused or not paying attention. So older people with hearing problems become more isolated and withdrawn because they feel left out.

The people mentioned in Jesus' parable may not have had presbycusis, but they had serious hearing problems. For some, the word never got in at all; they never heard it. Others had no hearing loss and the word got in, but it never got down into their hearts. They had accepted the gospel but the external pressures never let that word take root. A third group of hearers heard the word and let it take root, but 'the worries of this life, the deceitfulness of wealth and the desires for other things' choked the word (v. 19, NIV). Although they had the physical capacity for hearing, all three groups had hearing loss!

Older people may suffer from presbycusis, and doctors can provide help with their hearing loss. But hearing the gospel message and producing fruitful lives comes from a lifetime of providing good soil for the word. There are disciples who 'hear... accept... and bear fruit' (v. 20). Their lives reflect the fruit of the Spirit—'love, joy, peace, patience, kindness, generosity, faithfulness, gentleness, and self control' (Galatians 5:22–23).

REFLECTION

Are we allowing distractions of our time to choke out the word of God? Do we really hear God speak in our lives?

85

Mark 7:1–13

Adults and their Ageing Parents

For Moses said, 'Honour your father and your mother' ... But you say that if anyone tells father or mother, 'Whatever support you might have had from me is Corban' (that is, an offering to God)—then you no longer permit doing anything for a father or mother, thus making void the word of God through your tradition that you have handed on.

It seems as if 'Corban' may refer to an early example of some kind of trust fund, in which control of a person's property was turned over to the religious authorities on the condition that during one's lifetime one would continue to receive income from it. The purpose of the vow, as Jesus cited it, seemed to be specifically the non-support of parents.

Support that ought to have been for the parents was donated to the temple. Jesus sets over this tradition the ancient word of God that makes responsibility for parents of utmost significance. Jesus always showed concern for older parents. John reports that, even in his hour of agony, Jesus saw his mother standing with the beloved disciple and made provision for her care, thus fulfilling the traditional responsibility of the eldest son who had become head of the family (John 19:26–27).

Caring for ageing parents—learning how to confront the demands of caring for those who once took care of us—is no easy task. Care-givers often end up doing a dance between resentment and guilt. When care-givers give too much time to their older relative, they become tired and feel resentful. Reacting to this resentment, care-givers cut back on what they are giving and then feel guilty for what they are *not* doing for their relatives.

This episode from Jesus' ministry makes it clear that whatever the situation, adult children have a prior responsibility to care for ageing parents. No church work or community service can take the place of caring for parents. Nothing is sadder than to see families abandoning ageing parents or allowing one member to carry the burden.

Care-givers must find ways to help that do not burden their own lives. By setting realistic limits, by accepting help, and by learning how to rest, care-givers avoid the dance between resentment and guilt and offer constructive help for those who have entered the twilight of life.

THOUGHT

Lord, treat me tomorrow as I treat my ageing parents or relatives today.

86

MARK 9:2–13

A BRIEF VISION

Six days later, Jesus took with him Peter and James and John, and led them up a high mountain apart, by themselves. And he was transfigured before them... And there appeared to them Elijah with Moses, who were talking with Jesus. Then Peter said to Jesus, 'Rabbi, it is good for us to be here; let us make three dwellings, one for you, one for Moses, and one for Elijah.' He did not know what to say, for they were terrified.

Jeanne Calment, who lived to be 120 years old and was the oldest person whose birthday could be authenticated, was asked about her vision of the future. She replied, 'Very brief.' Every older person wonders about the future life. We may wonder about loved ones who have passed beyond this life, or about our own future. The gates guard their secrets well, and few stray beams of light escape through the crevices.

In this incredible moment on Mount Hermon, three disciples got a brief vision of heaven, the invisible reality surrounding earthly actuality. Jesus was transfigured before their eyes, resplendent with light. They became aware of two ghostly presences, Moses and Elijah. They were talking with Jesus about the 'exodus' that he would accomplish at

Jerusalem. The impulsive Peter blurted out that he wanted to build tabernacles for Jesus, Moses and Elijah. He wanted to cling to this moment of glory. But when they looked around, they saw no one any more, but only Jesus with themselves.

Campbell Morgan wrote:

It is evident that Peter, James, and John knew Moses and Elijah. How they knew them, of course, cannot be told. But the fact they knew them suggests that the identity of personality is maintained in the world that lies beyond, and in some wonderful manner, men know those whom here they have never known.[18]

The transfiguration of Jesus is a mystery that we do not understand but before which we worship. It assures us of resurrection life, and that, like Moses and Elijah, we will not just be resuscitated corpses but transformed persons. It also gives us hope for reunion with those 'angel faces whom we have loved long since, and lost awhile' (J.H. Newman). It reminds us of Paul's words, 'Eye has not seen, nor ear heard, nor have entered into the heart of man the things which God has prepared for those who love him (1 Corinthians 2:9, NKJV).

PRAYER

Jesus, you rose from the dead, not only to give us hope beyond the grave but to assure us that those who love the Lord will always meet again.

87

MARK 12:41-44

A WIDOW'S MIGHT

He sat down opposite the treasury, and watched the crowd putting money into the treasury. Many rich people put in large sums. A poor widow came and put in two small copper coins, which are worth a penny. Then he called his disciples and said to them, 'Truly I tell you, this poor widow has put in more than all those who are contributing to the treasury. For all of them have contributed out of their abundance; but she out of her poverty has put in everything she had, all she had to live on.'

Jesus had a special way to spot need which other people ignored. He saw the crippled woman in the synagogue (Luke 13:11); he sensed the woman in the crowd who clung to the hem of his garment (Mark 5:30); he reached out with compassion to the tormented man living in a graveyard and asked him, 'What is your name?' (Mark 5:9).

At the treasury, Jesus watched people come and go, bringing their money. He saw the rich subscribing large sums to the temple budget. (One wonders if their wealth was profit made from mortgages on widows' homes.) The eyes of his heart spied this poor widow who silently and secretly dropped in two measly copper coins, the smallest in the prevailing currency. What really got Jesus' attention was that she gave everything she had, 'all she had to live on'. The widow's mite became the widow's might! Her small gift was larger than all the rest, for even though she lived in poverty, she gave all she had.

Pearl was a poor widow who lived on a meagre pension. All she owned was a small flat. She told me that her major worry was not being able to stay in her own home, among the familiar pictures of her family and other mementos of her life. We had tried everything to get her to go to a nursing home, and when an older friend tried to persuade her to go, she replied, 'I'll be happy to visit you when you go!' Such determination and faith!

On one occasion when I visited her, she handed me her church offering and asked me to take it to the church. 'I just can't get out much any more,' she said, 'but I never forget my offering.'

My mind went back to that moment in the temple when the throngs were dropping their gifts of money into the offering receptacles, and Jesus singled out that widow.

PRAYER

Help me to realize, O Lord, that it is not how much I give to your kingdom that matters, but how much I have left after I have given.

88

LUKE 1:5–20 (NJB)

WHAT IF ZECHARIAH HAD RETIRED?

Then there appeared to him the angel of the Lord, standing on the right of the altar of incense. The sight disturbed Zechariah and he was overcome with fear. But the angel said to him, 'Zechariah, do not be afraid, for your prayer has been heard. Your wife Elizabeth is to bear you a son and you shall name him John…' Zechariah said to the angel, 'How can I know this? I am an old man and my wife is getting on in years.'

By the laws of Moses, Zechariah, the priest, should have retired at the age of fifty. However, he kept on with his duties in the sanctuary. An angel appeared to him, and told him that his prayer was answered. Zechariah did not believe the angel (v. 20), and lost his speech.

Perhaps his old age had made him reject what was unexpected. Even when he saw the angel's face and found that God had heard his prayer for a son, his mind was locked in the past. He could not accept the 'new'. For nine months the aged priest was silent. One woman commented that when Mary visited her aged relative, Elizabeth, in her sixth month, and two pregnant women began exchanging notes about their pregnancies, it was no wonder Zechariah was speechless!

Zechariah's silence was broken when he named his son John, 'God's gift'. As soon as he wrote the name, he too joined in the speech that praised God. His son would be the forerunner of the Messiah who would 'give light to those who sit in darkness and in the shadow of death, to guide our feet into the way of peace' (Luke 1:79).

Suppose Zechariah had turned his back on priesthood and retired to a quiet life in the hill country of Judah. He would have missed the many-splendoured appearance of an angel and the good news that God had answered his prayer for a son.

God still comes to older people with visions and dreams. If we capitulate to the hype of our culture that sees ageing only as a time for recreation and play, we too may miss the vision. Far too many older people conform to the fleeting fashions of the world and view old age as a time for playing bingo or for taking endless pleasure trips. God has something better for us, a purpose for these bonus years, and only as we spend time in the sanctuary, whether in a church or in the silent places of the heart, will we catch the vision.

MEDITATION

Find a quiet place either in a sanctuary or in your own home. Say a prayer, requesting that God make your later years full of meaning and enrichment. Expect God to answer.

89

LUKE 1:39–56

PREGNANT WOMEN ACROSS THE GENERATIONS

In those days Mary set out and went with haste to a Judean town in the hill country, where she entered the house of Zechariah and greeted Elizabeth. When Elizabeth heard Mary's greeting, the child leaped in her womb. And Elizabeth was filled with the Holy Spirit and exclaimed with a loud cry, 'Blessed are you among women, and blessed is the fruit of your womb.' ... And Mary remained with her about three months and then returned to her home.

Elizabeth, an older woman, held a honourable position in the Jewish community because she had descended from the priestly line of Aaron. As the wife of a priest, she was considered one of the most important women in Israel. She had everything going for her, except for one sorrow—she had no children. Jewish society considered children as wealth, and counted sons as old-age insurance. Elizabeth was barren and too old to have children.

Then the impossible became a reality and she became pregnant. For five months she remained in seclusion (Luke

1:24), and shortly thereafter her kinswoman, Mary, came to visit Elizabeth at her home. Elizabeth learned not only that Mary was with child, but also that Mary's child would be the Messiah. This older woman had a depth of spiritual wisdom by becoming the first person to acknowledge Mary as the mother of the Messiah. She understood what God was doing in Mary: Mary was pregnant with the chosen Son.

For three months these pregnant women stayed together, sharing their thoughts and feelings, talking about what God had done. Elizabeth, the older woman, became the mentor and spiritual friend of Mary, the younger woman.

Author John O'Donohue points out that in the Celtic tradition, there is a beautiful understanding of love and friendship. The old Gaelic term for this is *anam cara*, 'soul friend'. With the *anam cara* you can share your innermost self, your mind and your heart. The soul friend enables you to be understood without any conditions. 'Love allows understanding to dawn, and understanding is precious. When you are understood you are home... When you really feel understood, you feel free to release yourself into the trust and shelter of the other person's soul.'[19] This is the relationship that Mary and Elizabeth shared for three months, as the older woman became an *anam cara* for the younger woman chosen by God.

PRAYER

Lord, bless me with a soul friend!

90

LUKE 2:22–38

THE REWARDS OF PATIENT WAITING

Now there was a man in Jerusalem whose name was Simeon; this man was righteous and devout, looking forward to the consolation of Israel, and the Holy Spirit rested on him... Guided by the Spirit, Simeon came into the temple; and when the parents brought in the child Jesus... Simeon took him in his arms and praised God... There was also a prophet, Anna... She was of a great age, having lived with her husband seven years after her marriage, then as a widow to the age of eighty-four... At that moment she came, and began to praise God and to speak about the child to all who were looking for the redemption of Jerusalem.

Two old saints, Simeon and Anna, had waited for years for this moment. Simeon was a just and righteous man waiting to see the Messiah. He had received a special insight that he would not die before he had seen and recognized the Messiah. Anna was 84 years old, constantly worshipping God in the temple. Matthew Henry speculated that Anna had an apartment funded by temple charities. She never missed a service. After all these years of meeting other people's needs, you would think that Anna had earned the right to rest. But she waited actively without interrupting her service.

It is hard to imagine their joy when they saw Mary and Joseph and the young baby and knew that this was God's anointed one. Their weary bones were suddenly filled with joy. Their long years of waiting for the Messiah had ended, and the moment had come. Simeon took the baby in his arms and blessed him. 'My eyes have seen your salvation, which you have prepared in the presence of all peoples, a light for revelation to the Gentiles and for glory to your people Israel' (vv. 30–32). As he looked at the baby's mother, his joy was mingled with sadness—'A sword will pierce your own soul too' (v. 35)—as if he seemed to know the pain that lay ahead.

Anna confirmed what Simeon had said, and realized that this baby was God's anointed one. She did not keep the gift to herself, but turned around to the crowds to explain their redemption (v. 38).

Anna and Simeon set a fine example as older persons waiting for Jesus' coming into their own hearts and into the hearts of humanity. As older people, we too could ask God that we might not experience death until we have seen Jesus closely in our own thoughts and in the faces of people whom we serve.

PRAYER

Lord, thank you for the examples of two older people, Anna and Simeon. Grant me patience to find Christ in the face of others.

LUKE 2:25–38

TWO OLD FRIENDS

Now there was a man in Jerusalem whose name was Simeon; this man was righteous and devout, looking forward to the consolation of Israel... There was also a prophet, Anna the daughter of Phanuel, of the tribe of Asher. She was of a great age, having lived with her husband seven years after her marriage, then as a widow to the age of eighty-four. She never left the temple but worshipped there with fasting and prayer night and day.

When Jesus first touched the eyes of the blind man at Bethsaida, he asked, 'Can you see anything?' And the man looked up and said, 'I see people, but they look like trees, walking' (Mark 8:23–24). How many times I have read the story of Anna and Simeon in the temple on that day when Mary and Joseph brought the baby Jesus. But only recently did I see that Anna and Simeon were old friends! Surely they knew each other, for they both spent many hours in the temple. Luke tells us that Anna 'never left the temple but worshipped there with fasting and prayer night and day'.

Anna's past included a major tragedy—early widowhood, after being married only seven years. Nothing else is known about Simeon, except that he was old and believed he would see the Messiah before he died. We can only speculate whether they had been friends before the encounter with Mary and Joseph and the baby. But we can be sure that they became friends, bound now by their common belief that God had indeed fulfilled his promise in bringing consolation to Israel.

Tracy Kidder's novel *Two Old Friends* (Houghlin Mifflin, 1993) tells of the friendship between Lou Freed and Joe Torchio, strangers thrust together as roommates in Linda Manor, a nursing home. It was there that they were relegated to live out their final years with the old, or as the old. In that place there was little communication between residents, and most simply lived out their days in isolation and desolation. Lou and Joe developed a friendship that transcended all the indignities and impersonal life of a nursing home. Most of the residents in Linda Manor sat in hallways or rooms, staying by themselves and maintaining their differences. Lou and Joe became friends, sharing their days and rejoicing in their differences, and taking the sting out of institutional life with a vibrant outlook on life. Older people need such friends upon whom they can depend and so gain support.

REFLECTION

Who is my old friend now? How can I develop and nourish old friends?

92

LUKE 7:11-17

COMPASSION KNEELS AND CARES

Soon afterwards he went to a town called Nain, and his disciples and a large crowd went with him. As he approached the gate of the town, a man who had died was being carried out. He was his mother's only son, and she was a widow... When the Lord saw her, he had compassion for her and said to her, 'Do not weep.' Then he came forward and touched the bier, and the bearers stood still. And he said, 'Young man, I say to you, rise!' The dead man sat up and began to speak, and Jesus gave him to his mother.

Every so often my mundane life is interrupted by a funeral procession, a strong reminder that death is always present. We may push aside this common anxiety with activities and diversions of every conceivable kind. Yet, however suppressed, it lurks in our midst, ready to leap out at any moment. Just when we think we're safest, death strikes a friend or loved one.

Jesus came near the gate of the city of Nain, 25 miles from Capernaum. He met a funeral procession. A widow's only son had died and he was being carried on a bier to the grave. In the front of the procession were the professional wailing women, then the mourners, then the bier, and then a crowd of men and boys.

Widows in that day were pitiable in any case, for they had no legal rights and could not receive any legal inheritance. They were dependent on their sons or the relatives of their husbands, whose support could not be legally binding. The death of her only son left this widow defenceless in a cruel world. With no male heir, the family name would be cut off in Israel.

Jesus stopped the procession with a gesture. He brought that screaming, shrieking mob to a silent halt. Then with a quiet authority Jesus spoke to the young man in the bier and called him back from death. The young man sat up—Luke uses the medical word which is regularly used of a patient sitting up in bed—and began to speak. Jesus then gave the son back to his mother. William Barclay says that Jesus used his power, 'not to glorify himself, not to gain prestige and fame, but to give a son back to his mother'.[20]

When Jesus saw the widow, he had compassion for her and felt her grief. It is interesting that in the Gospels the particularly strong Greek word used here for 'compassion' is never used in relation to anyone except Jesus. Our compassion must go beyond pity to action.

MEDITATION
Pity stands and stares. Compassion kneels and cares.

93

LUKE 15:11–32

THE WAITING OLD MAN

But while [the son] was still yet far off, his father saw him and was filled with compassion; he ran and put his arms around him and kissed him… The father said to his slaves, 'Quickly, bring out a robe—the best one—and put it on him; put a ring on his finger and sandals on his feet… for this son of mine was dead and is alive again; he was lost and is found! … Then the father said to [the elder son], 'Son, you are always with me, and all that is mine is yours.'

There is no doubt that the central figure in this parable is the father, the old man. First he graciously received the younger son who had wasted his life, felt beaten down and didn't expect much except judgment. The father saw the son from a distance and rushed out to wrap his arms around him, as the son walked through the village and heard the cat-calls and jeers of the villagers. How often the eyes of the old man had looked towards the horizon, seeking his son. He had never forgotten him or given him up. He threw aside all dignity and ran to him. He didn't ask where he had been or demand an accounting of those lost years, nor did he punish him for his failures. He just surrounded him with love and signs of sonship.

But the old man also loved his elder son who had worked all his life and stayed at home. If the younger son was the rebel, the older was the dutiful son who had done all the right things. Although the elder son resented the prodigal, and couldn't understand why his brother couldn't be like him, the old man still loved him. He told him, 'Son, all that is mine is yours.' It is much easier to love a penitent son than one who is stubborn and hard-hearted, and yet the old man's love is there for him.

We have unanswered questions as the parable ends. Did the younger son really repent or did he go back to the far country? Did he influence his older brother to leave home? Did the elder son ever swallow his pride and become reconciled to his family? Why is the prodigal's mother never mentioned? Was she dead?

The story ends, however, with celebration. The major focus is on the old man, whose prodigal love for both of his sons is an unveiling of the love of God, the infinite grace and tenderness of the old man's heart.

What a role model for all older Christians to emulate, in this unconditional love that the father had for his sons.

REFLECTION
For the love of God is broader
Than the measures of the mind;
And the heart of the Eternal
Is most wonderfully kind.
FREDERICK WILLIAM FABER (1814–63)

94

BEST... UNTIL LAST

When the steward tasted the water that had become wine, and did not know where it came from (though the servants who had drawn the water knew), the steward called the bridegroom and said to him, 'Everyone serves the good wine first, and then the inferior wine after the guests have become drunk. But you have kept the good wine until now.' Jesus did this, the first of his signs, in Cana of Galilee, and revealed his glory.

At first we question why Jesus performed this miracle at Cana. Unlike so many of Jesus' miracles, which have a fairly simple justification in compassion for the unfortunate, this miracle is different. It is one thing to heal a leper or bring hope to the sick, but to create 150 gallons of wine to quench the thirst of wedding guests seems somewhat trivial.

We find the reason for the miracle in verse 11. 'Jesus did this, the first of his signs, in Cana of Galilee, and revealed his glory.' It was Jesus' first public act, in which he was saying that he would transform things, that a new day was dawning and the kingdom of God was at hand. Some commentators argue that those six stone jars of water represented the Jewish rites of purification, whose significance would change radically with the new wine of the gospel. John sees beyond the obvious to the deeper meaning of this story. It is not just that Jesus turned water into wine at a wedding feast to save the host from the embarrassment because the supply of wine to accommodate unexpected guests had run out. The family and the young couple would never have lived down the shame of it. Hospitality in the East was a sacred duty.

The miracle at Cana was also a sign that when Jesus enters a person's life there comes a new exhilaration, like water turning into wine. What does this mean for older people? It is significant that the steward tells the bridegroom, 'You have kept the good wine until now.' The best wine was served last. So often, life for older people can become terribly boring and flat. When we lose our work identity, we may also lose interest in life, and there is a vague dissatisfaction in all of life. But the best wine is kept until last. Jesus turns the water of old Judaism into the new wine of his kingdom. To live with him is to have the great adventure and the new exhilaration—at any age!

REFLECTION
Grow old along with me!
The best is yet to be,
The last of life, for which
The first was made.

ROBERT BROWNING (1812–89)

95

JOHN 3:1–16 (NIV)

BEING BORN AGAIN... WHEN OLD

Now there was a man of the Pharisees named Nicodemus, a member of the Jewish ruling council. He came to Jesus at night... In reply Jesus declared, 'I tell you the truth, no one can see the kingdom of God unless he is born again.' 'How can a man be born when he is old?' Nicodemus asked... Jesus answered, 'I tell you the truth, no one can enter the kingdom of God unless he is born of water and the Spirit.'

Author and social worker Vivian E. Greenberg says, 'It is a fact that currently more people over 65 are entering psycho-therapy than ever before... For the truth is that we grow and learn for as long as we live; that contrary to popular opinion, old men and old women can and do change.'[21]

Nicodemus came to Jesus at night. He was a member of the Sanhedrin, no doubt a wealthy, powerful, rich old man. He showed his age when he asked Jesus, 'How can a man be born when he is old?' Although he had all the marks of success and power, his life lacked something. He must have had questions like these: 'Why do I feel this deep loneliness? Why haven't all the good things in my life brought satisfaction? Why is there still an anxious uneasiness in my life?' Nicodemus

needed a rabbi, a mentor, a sage to look at the main themes of his life and to plumb beneath the surface for deeper layers of meaning.

Jesus became his spiritual director. He confronted Nicodemus with his need for rebirth by the Spirit and helped him to realize that all the achievements of his life must now pale in significance beside a new birth which would come 'from above'. Just then, perhaps, a gust of wind began to whistle outside in the dark night, and Jesus said that being born again was like that. It wasn't something you did. The wind did it. The Spirit did it. It would transform life.

Later on, when Jesus was dead, Nicodemus went along with Joseph of Arimathea to pay his last respects at the tomb in broad daylight (John 19:38–42). Nothing else is known of Nicodemus in the biblical record. But there is reason to believe that he became a follower of Jesus and later experienced a new birth of the Spirit.

The story of Nicodemus reminds us that new birth can occur for older people. People over 65 not only change but change faster. They know that there is less time to find the meaning of life and to become right with God. The Spirit can bring new birth at any age!

PRAYER
'Create in me a clean heart, O God, and put a new and right spirit within me' (Psalm 51:10).

96

JOHN 16:25-33

ALONE, BUT NOT LONELY

Jesus answered them, 'Do you now believe? The hour is coming, indeed it has come, when you will be scattered, each to his home, and you will leave me alone. Yet I am not alone because the Father is with me. I have said this to you, so that in me you may have peace. In the world you face persecution. But take courage; I have conquered the world!'

When Jesus spoke these words he was moments away from the terrible loneliness of his last hours of agony on this earth. Jesus walked that lonesome valley, alone, yet he was not alone, for the Father's strong presence was with him.

For many people, coping with old age means coping with the problems of loneliness. For widows and widowers, the fearful awareness of being alone often leads to depression. There are moments when there may be nobody to turn to but God. Then it is good to remember that Jesus understands what loneliness means, for no one tasted the agony of loneliness more than Christ in the garden of Gethsemane, and nobody tasted isolation more than Christ at the cross.

A British film, *The Whisperers*, confronted this issue of older people living alone. An old lady, played by Dame Edith Evans, lives alone in a small flat. Her lawless son returns home long enough to hide stolen cash in the flat, and because of that she is robbed and beaten. The welfare people think it would be best if her husband, who had deserted her years ago, would return to live with her. He does return, but it becomes evident that the situation won't work out, so he leaves again. The old lady returns to her empty flat and smiles at the drip, drip, drip of a leaking tap. Suddenly, the audience is struck with the realization that it is better to live surrounded by friendly inanimate objects than to live among incompatible human beings.

Many older people live alone with courage and dignity. They discover that the emptiness of feeling alone can open their hearts and make them more perceptive of the presence of God, who speaks in the silence. A gregarious American tourist climbed a high mountain in the Himalayas to meet an old guru who lived there. Seeing that he was all alone, the American asked, 'Aren't you lonely up here?' Slowly the old guru replied, 'No, not until you came!' Older people cherish companionship, but being alone can be a blessing, too.

MEDITATION

Spend a few minutes by yourself, and ask God to speak to you in the silence. With his presence, you are never alone.

97

JOHN 21:15–19 (NJB)

THAT DAY MAY COME

Jesus said to [Peter], 'Feed my sheep. In all truth I tell you, when you were young you put on your own belt and walked where you liked; but when you grow old you will stretch out your hands, and somebody else will put a belt round you and take where you would rather not go.'

If ever there are words in scripture that speak to older people, it is these words of Jesus to Peter. Although Jesus was referring to the martyrdom of Peter, when Roman hands would bind Peter and nail him to a cross, they speak to older people suffering another kind of slow death. How many times I have thought of Jesus' words as I wandered down the endless halls of nursing homes, or visited those who must rely on hired and often indifferent help to feed and clean them.

When we think about our future, we shy away from picturing ourselves in a nursing home. That is one place we would rather not go to. Nursing homes can be scary places, and the best we can hope for is that we will not end our days in these tribal villages. It is a frightening prospect for one who has spent a lifetime fighting to be in control, to lose that control suddenly. It is a terrible thought that the day may come when someone else 'will put a belt around us', take us from here to there, and care for our most humble bodily needs.

The reality is that that day may well come, as we live longer in the 21st century. No one knows what lies in store for us at the end of life, but if we must live with a chronic illness such as painful osteoarthritis or the damaging effects of Alzheimer's, or the aftermath of a stroke, we know that a greater level of care will be required. For some it may be possible to stay in their own homes with the help of care-givers. For others it will mean going to specialist care centres or hospitals for that kind of care.

But Jesus said to Peter, 'Follow me', and that road led to a painful death on a cross. The historian Eusebius tells us that when the moment of crucifixion came, Peter requested that he might be crucified head downwards, for he was not worthy to die as his Lord had died (*Ecclesiastical History*, 3.1). Peter followed with courage. If our life should end in a nursing home, we can be assured of Christ's loving presence there, and what we perceived as a place of despair can become a time of soul growth and authentic living.

PRAYER

Lord, if it be your will that I go to a nursing home, give me grace to find a home there.

98

ACTS 1:12–14

MARY: MOTHER OF THE INFANT CHURCH

Then they returned to Jerusalem from the mount called Olivet, which is near Jerusalem, a sabbath day's journey away. When they had entered the city, they went to the room upstairs where they were staying, Peter, and John, and James, and Andrew, Philip and Thomas, Bartholomew and Matthew, James son of Alphaeus, and Simon the Zealot, and Judas son of James. All these were constantly devoting themselves to prayer, together with certain women, including Mary the mother of Jesus, as well as his brothers.

This is the last mention of Mary, the mother of Jesus, in the scriptures. Yet it is an important one. She was in the upper room with the disciples, before the day of Pentecost came. Mary behaved in the upper room as she behaved in the stable at Bethlehem. There she cared for the infant Jesus; in Jerusalem she nurtured the infant Church.

Although she disappears from the pages of scripture, tradition claims that she lived in the house of John at Ephesus, since Jesus had entrusted her care to John at the cross: "'Woman, here is your son.' Then he said to the disciple,

"Here is your mother"' (John 19:26–27). In that moment, Jesus formed the new humanity, based not on blood ties but on a common relationship to him. Many scholars believe that Mary visited Paul in prison at Caesarea and became a living source for Luke's account of Jesus' life. She must have shared with Luke those precious memories of Jesus' birth that she had treasured in her heart, as well as other reflections on her son.

It is hard to think of Jesus as an old man, bruised with the years, dying in senility on the cross, his last gasp being the gasp of an old man. But we know that Jesus must have experienced some of the agonies of old age at the cross. He stumbled and fell under the weight of the cross, knew the agony of abandonment, and died alone.

But Mary died in old age and lived out her life in full, under the divinely assigned care of John. No doubt she became the matriarch of the infant Church, the mother of all who loved her Son. In her own way, Mary became the purest expression of how to grow old, balancing time between deep contemplation and actively encouraging the infant Church.

PRAYER

My life is an instant,
An hour which passes by;
My life is a moment
Which I have no power to stay.
You know, O my God,
That to love you here on earth
I have only today.

THÉRÈSE OF LISIEUX (1873–97)

99

ACTS 4:32–37; 9:26–30

BARNABAS: HE KEPT HIS HARNESS ON

There was a Levite, a native of Cyprus, Joseph, to whom the apostles gave the name Barnabas (which means 'son of encouragement'). He sold a field that belonged to him, then brought the money, and laid it at the apostles' feet... When [Saul] had come to Jerusalem, he attempted to join the disciples; and they were all afraid of him... But Barnabas took him, brought him to the apostles, and described for them how on the road he had seen the Lord.

In the old days of horse and carriage, an old horse was taken away from his work of drawing a carriage, and his owners took off his harness for the last time. The old horse would go back to the stable to spend the rest of his days resting, eating, sleeping and dreaming the sort of dreams horses have.

Not so Joseph of Cyprus. He kept his harness on, as he became a major player in the drama of the early Church. When he became a Christian, he sold his land and gave the money to the Jerusalem apostles. It was Barnabas who stood alone in accepting and encouraging Saul of Tarsus when the former oppressor came to Jerusalem and claimed to have seen the light. We can identify with the apostles in their fear of Saul, for only recently he had unleashed a persecution against the young Church. When the doors seemed closed against the risk of Saul's presence in the Church, Barnabas chanced his own place and reputation. He became the mediator who opened the doors of the Church to its former persecutor and welcomed Saul into the fellowship.

Barnabas and Saul brought money from Antioch to Jerusalem when the church there was suffering a great famine (Acts 11:27–30). On the first missionary journey, John Mark went home. Barnabas wanted to take John Mark with them on another journey, but Paul unilaterally vetoed the suggestion (Acts 15:38). This caused a sharp disagreement between Paul and Barnabas, and their partnership in the gospel dissolved. Barnabas once again took the side of a maligned colleague. As he had done for Paul, he gave the deserter another chance and saved him from sure disgrace and disuse. Indeed, one wonders if John Mark would ever have penned the earliest Gospel if it had not been for the encouragement of Barnabas.

Surely, Barnabas is a model for older church members to emulate, to stay in the harness and continue to give their all.

PRAYER

Help us, O Christ, to have the spirit of encouragement that was in Barnabas as we serve you in the Church.

100

ACTS 5:33–42

A WORD OF WISDOM

When they heard this, they were enraged and wanted to kill them. But a Pharisee in the council named Gamaliel, a teacher of the law, respected by all the people, stood up and ordered the men to be put outside for a short time. Then he said to them, '…So in the present case, I tell you, keep away from these men and let them alone; because if this plan or this undertaking is of human origin, it will fail; but if it is of God, you will not be able to overthrow them—in that case you may even be found fighting against God!'

How many times in the life of the Church is a word of wisdom needed! Often heated words provoke conflict, and sharp differences are only exacerbated by lengthy tirades in church councils. Opponents on both sides of controversial issues display a self-righteousness that implies that they alone are right. How different the calm, rational wisdom of Gamaliel, an honoured Pharisaic member of the Sanhedrin, who advocated caution in the treatment of Peter and the other disciples. The Sadducees wanted extreme measures taken against the disciples, and undoubtedly if it had not been for Gamaliel's intervention the apostles would have been executed that very day. Gamaliel's argument was simple: if Jesus was a false prophet, as others had been, the movement would soon fade into oblivion. If, however, the work was 'of God', no one could stop them. Was Gamaliel simply playing politics in his wish to protect Pharisaic Judaism, or did he sense in the events he had witnessed the power and purpose of God? We do not know.

Gamaliel's wisdom proved prophetic. If the Sanhedrin had taken more extreme measures against the Christians, they would have been fighting God. History later proved the vindication of the disciples.

In the councils and courts of the Church, we need that balanced judgment, careful weighing of evidence and a willingness not to act rashly. Gamaliel was not impulsive or quick to dismiss the disciples. He had the perspective to be far-sighted about the future and let God be the judge. If this movement is of human origin, it will fail. But if it is of God, it will succeed.

REFLECTION
In necessary things, unity;
In doubtful things, liberty;
In all things, charity.
'Motto', Richard Baxter (1615–91)

101

ACTS 9:36–43 (NIV)

LITTLE THINGS DO MATTER

In Joppa there was a disciple named Tabitha (which, when translated, is Dorcas), who was always doing good and helping the poor. About that time she became sick and died, and her body was washed and placed in an upstairs room. Lydda was near Joppa; so when the disciples heard that Peter was in Lydda, they sent two men to him and urged him, 'Please come at once!' Peter went with them, and when he arrived he was taken upstairs to the room. All the widows stood around him, crying and showing him the robes and other clothing that Dorcas had made while she was still with them.

Tabitha's particular ministry was aiding a group of widows as a seamstress, and she also most likely offered companionship and comfort. Whatever her role, she was 'always doing good and helping the poor'. When Dorcas died, some disciples heard that Peter was nearby and they sent him an urgent message to come without delay. When Peter entered the upper room, all the widows stood by weeping. They held up the many garments and other clothing Tabitha had made for them while she was living. Peter raised Tabitha from the dead, and then called the saints and widows and showed them their friend.

Tabitha is the only New Testament person raised from the dead by a disciple of Jesus. The Greek word for 'disciple' used to describe Tabitha is *matheria*, a female disciple. This is the only time the word is used in the New Testament.

This story of Dorcas, a humble dressmaker and doer of good works in Joppa, seems to sneak into the stirring story of the early Church in the book of Acts. Yet it is a reminder that small deeds of kindness and mercy in the name of Christ do matter. Small things constitute the whole of life. We do not always have to do great things, to have extraordinary experiences every day, or to produce major changes. Sometimes small things such as dressmaking for widows can be major acts of Christian love and kindness. Often these are the deeds that are never forgotten. British historian E.L. Woodward once wrote, 'Everything good has to be done over and over again, for ever.' (source?)

REFLECTION

Tabitha made time to do what she could for others. List some loving acts you would do for older people if you had all the time in the world. Then do at least one thing on your list this week.

102

ROMANS 8:18–25

WHEN THERE'S HOPE, THERE'S LIFE

We know that the whole creation has been groaning in labour pains until now; and not only the creation, but we ourselves, who have the first fruits of the Spirit, groan inwardly while we wait for adoption, the redemption of our bodies. For in hope we were saved. Now hope that is seen is not hope. For who hopes for what is seen? But if we hope for what we do not see, we wait for it with patience.

The Shawshank Redemption is a film about friendship in a depressing prison setting. Every kind of brutality operates in that prison. One day, a prisoner who is working in the library manages to get into the main office, finds a wonderful piece of classical music, a duet from Mozart's *The Marriage of Figaro*, and plays it on the loudspeaker into the prison yard. As from eternal spheres, this beautiful music falls on all those haunted lives in that dreary place. Prisoners stop in their tracks and listen. An eerie silence fills that prison yard, as if, in the lovely shock of the music's beauty, the lost grandeur of creation is suddenly present and a moment of hope is born.

Instead of lamenting the injustices done to him in and outside of prison, Paul sings of a hope that kept him going:

'But if we hope for what we do not see, we wait for it with patience.'

Many older people suffer from depression, some of which is linked with hopelessness. Worries about financial resources, family health, responsibilities—worry about everything—becomes exaggerated in depression. Older people become obsessed with worry and ruminate continually. It is all too easy to give up and surrender to despair.

Older people need a ministry of hope. Hope is not a Pollyanna optimism or a wish for better things to come. It is not a vague longing that the future will always be better. Hope is not passive. It is a sense of possibility, in situations of limitation and discouragement. It is the sense of a way out and a destiny still to be realized. Hope is what enables us to say 'yes' to life in spite of limitations. An older man, suffering from cancer of the liver, kept repeating to his friends, 'There is always hope!'

Older people need hope, for where there is hope there is life. When despair over lingering illnesses or other threats to our well-being come along, patient hope can be a way through the dark moments.

PRAYER

Loving God, when life closes in, and everything seems so dismal and dark, help me not to give up hope that it will one day be better.

103

ROMANS 12:9–21 (NKJV)

IT TAKES A LONG TIME TO BECOME YOUNG

Let love be without hypocrisy. Abhor what is evil. Cling to what is good. Be kindly affectionate to one another with brotherly love, in honour giving preference to one another; not lagging in diligence, fervent in spirit, serving the Lord; rejoicing in hope, patient in tribulation, continuing steadfastly in prayer.

It is regrettable that some stereotypes of older people persist in a culture still obsessed with youth: older people are thought to be physically unattractive, or burdens on society. No wonder many younger people view getting old as a capital punishment and ageing as the shipwreck of their lives. However, many older people have a youthful spirit, full of exuberance and vitality. There is a sparkle in their presence and a lilt in their steps, and something in their old bodies that is incredibly young. Conversely, there are many young people who are gloomy, grave and depressing, sounding like some 90-year-olds.

Paul is calling the Roman Christians to give witness to their faith, and among the qualities of that witness is being 'fervent in spirit'. This youthful spirit does not depend on outward circumstances but on a quality of soul. Time makes us old, but there is a place in the soul that time cannot touch. In later life, every Christian is called to soulful ageing, to maintain that youthful spirit.

In 1966, a retrospective of the artist Picasso's works in chronological sequence was exhibited at Cannes. Hundreds of paintings, from the first that Picasso produced as an adolescent beginner to the latest paintings of the 85-year-old master, lined the walls. The first paintings were conventional landscapes and still lifes. A little further on, the landscapes changed, taking on new colours. The last paintings exhibited a free spirit, culminating in an explosion of never-before-seen colours and shapes and visions. Picasso himself roamed the gallery and enjoyed the show more than anyone. A woman stopped him one day and said, 'I don't understand. Over there—the beginning works, so solemn and serious. Then the later ones, so different, colourful, irrepressible. It seems as if they should be reversed, starting there with your new works and ending there with the first.' Picasso replied, 'Madam, it takes a long time to become young!'

PRAYER

Spirit of God, fill us with your Spirit regardless of our age or our state in life. May our lives be so Spirit-filled that no one will dread getting old.

104

1 CORINTHIANS 13

LOVE WILL FIND A WAY

If I speak in the tongues of mortals and of angels, but do not have love, I am a noisy gong or a clanging cymbal. And if I have prophetic powers, and understand all mysteries and all knowledge, and if I have all faith, so as to remove mountains, but do not have love, I am nothing. If I give away all my possessions, and if I hand over my body so that I may boast, but do not have love, I gain nothing.

The *New Yorker* magazine had a striking cartoon on a recent cover. It showed an elderly gentleman standing in pyjamas and dressing-gown at his apartment door. He had just secured the door with several locks. Only as he shot home two heavy bolts did he notice a small, white envelope stuck beneath the door. On the envelope was a large sticker in the shape of a heart. A little child who lived down the hall had broken through his security system with a Valentine. Love found a way.

For many older people, love remains the most excellent way. Paul had written the poem of 1 Corinthians 13 and polished it many times. When he wrote to the divided, quarrelsome church at Corinth, he knew that this was the very slot for it. Even now it holds a special meaning for older people who need God's love in a special way.

At a worship service I led in a nursing home, communication with the residents seemed impossible. Most had hearing problems and many were stroke victims. No words would communicate God's love. So we sang the old song, 'Love lifted me... when nothing else could help, love lifted me.' We joined hands and hugged each other in a sacrament of touch. Love broke through the barrier of age in that place and brought new life.

Late in life, the renowned scientist Henry Drummond wrote, 'You will find as you look back on your life, that the moments that stand out, the moments when you have really lived, the moments when you have done great things, are the moments you have done things in a spirit of love.'[22] As we grow older, we know that many values we thought important when we were young no longer seem so important. Only faith, hope and love remain. And the greatest of these still is love. Centuries ago, Jesus of Nazareth said, 'Love one another' (John 13:34). That remains.

REFLECTION

Read 1 Corinthians 13 again and again and let it grip your imagination and fire your soul. Read and practise it.

105

1 CORINTHIANS 15:35–58

RAISED IN GLORY

But someone will ask, 'How are the dead raised? With what kind of body do they come?' Fool! What you sow does not come to life unless it dies. And as for what you sow, you do not sow the body that is to be, but a bare seed, perhaps of wheat or of some other grain. But God gives it a body as he has chosen, and to each kind of seed its own body… So it is with the resurrection of the dead. What is sown is perishable, what is raised is imperishable. It is sown in dishonour, it is raised in glory. It is sown a physical body, it is raised a spiritual body.

The process of ageing is like farming. There are inherent cycles from life to death, and during the latter years our seasons emerge. Farmers renew their fields with fresh, new crops in the spring. When people reach retirement age, they have opportunity to renew their lives. In the second season, summer, growth and nurturing occur. Older adults need support and direction as they struggle to change life patterns ingrained for years.

The third stage is one of gathering and harvesting. Older people find autumn as a time to harvest their rich experiences. Finally, winter comes, a season of rest and death. After the crops are gathered and preserved, the plants wither and die. The field is left to rest until the next cycle of seasons begins. However, the dying plants leave seeds behind them that will be the source of new plants.

Paul used the world of nature to tell about the spiritual body. As a seed of corn or wheat is put in the ground and dies, it springs into new life as a fully developed plant. Sown as a 'physical body' in the spring of life, the body of the Christian becomes a 'spiritual body' in the resurrection life. Whatever else this means, it must mean, at least, the continuance of personality and individuality. This new spiritual body will be imperishable, glorious and powerful, and will bear the mark of the man of heaven, Jesus Christ.

Paul makes it abundantly clear that his confidence about the future is not based on any theory of human nature; it is rooted and grounded on his faith in God. God who raised the Lord Jesus Christ in that explosive joyful experience will raise us in victory with him. 'But thanks be to God, who gives us the victory through our Lord Jesus Christ' (v. 57).

REFLECTION

As you remember loved ones whom you have loved long since, and lost awhile, ponder these words.

> O Lord of life, where'er they be,
> Safe in Your own eternity,
> Now live Your children gloriously.
> Alleluia! Alleluia! Alleluia!
>
> FREDERICK LUCIAN HOSMER (1840–1929)

106

2 CORINTHIANS 4:16–18

PAUL'S VIEW OF AGEING

So we do not lose heart. Even though our outer nature is wasting away, our inner nature is being renewed day by day. For this slight momentary affliction is preparing us for an eternal weight of glory beyond all measure, because we look not at what can be seen but what cannot be seen; for what can be seen is temporary, but what cannot be seen is eternal.

When Paul wrote these words, he was an older person. Physically, every day he was growing older and weaker, and yet inwardly, spiritually, he kept for ever young. Paul knew that there is something which indeed is destroyed, and must be accepted—our physical strength, our need for action in the broader world. But that does not mean resigning from the world but being a presence in the world. The inner man is being renewed every day; life is different, but it is still fully life.

This remarkable insight from the apostle Paul is confirmed in many creative older people. Indeed, the buoyancy of spirit increases in some older persons as if in direct proportion to the decrease of physical energy. Even the loss of work and independence does not curtail the spirit in creative ageing.

People with a sense of spiritual well-being seem to be full of life, and they value every day.

Paul's words challenge the culture in which we live. It is the most common assumption of our Western culture that life has a peak, with an upward and downward slope on either side. No matter to what age we assign the 'prime of life', we see the later years as decline coming after it. But for Paul, even the realistic losses of older age do not mean the end of growth. His life view is that we are always moving forward, and the spirit can be renewed day by day. Life is more than a decline into death; it is growth in the spirit. So, without denying the losses that occur in ageing, growth in the spirit means that all of life is prime time.

There was once a young woman who visited the studio of the great artist Michelangelo. She was grieved to see him hacking away at the beautiful marble and argued with the illustrious sculptor about what he was wasting. She pointed to the pile of chips that littered the floor. But Michelangelo said, 'The more the marble wastes, the more the statue grows.' The years may hack away at the beauty of our bodies, but each part that time takes away reveals the beauty of an inner spirit.

PRAYER

Give me grace, O loving God, to realize that even when old age hacks away at my body, my inner person can be renewed.

107

2 CORINTHIANS 5:1–10

GOD'S HOUSING SCHEME FOR OLDER PERSONS

For we know that if the earthly tent we live in is destroyed, we have a building from God, a house not made with hands, eternal in the heavens… So we are always confident; even though we know that while we are at home in the body we are away from the Lord—for we walk by faith, not by sight.

John Quincy Adams, former US President, was 80 years old and met a friend on the street. 'Good morning,' said the friend, 'and how is John Quincy Adams today?'

'Thank you,' the ex-President replied, 'John Quincy Adams himself is well, quite well. But the house in which he lives at present is becoming dilapidated. It is tottering upon its foundation. Time and the seasons have nearly destroyed it. Its roof is pretty well worn out. The walls are much shattered, and it trembles with every wind. The old tenement is becoming almost uninhabitable, and I think John Quincy Adams will have to move out of it soon. But he himself is quite well, quite well.'

Paul compares the difference between this life and the next

to the difference between living in a tent and in a house. The tent is temporary; it is made temporary on purpose, since it has to be portable. But a house is built to last. Paul was a tent-maker, and he knew what he was talking about. A person who lives in a tent never belongs where he is; he always belongs somewhere else. A man who lives in a house belongs there. Paul says, 'While we are still in this tent, we groan under our burden' (2 Corinthians 5:4). Our bodies, like tottering tents, will age according to processes we cannot alter or reverse (despite the advances of medical technology and cosmetics). But God has prepared a new home for us in heaven. No wonder Jesus used this analogy when he said to the disciples shortly before his death, 'In my Father's house there are many dwelling places' (John 14:2).

Although our bodies, the houses we live in now, may get old and crumble, our souls are ever young and buoyant, awaiting our new homes in a better life.

REFLECTION

Meditate on these words of the Christian mystic, Meister Eckhart (?1260–1327):

My soul is as young as the day it was created.
Yes, and much younger! In fact, I am younger today
than I was yesterday, and if I am not younger tomorrow
than I am today, I would be ashamed of myself.
People who dwell in God dwell in the eternal now;
there, people can never grow old.

MATTHEW FOX (TRS.), *MEDITATIONS WITH MEISTER ECKHART* (BEAR, 1983), P. 32

108

2 CORINTHIANS 12:1–10

BLESSINGS IN DISGUISE

Therefore, to keep me from being too elated, a thorn was given me in the flesh, a messenger of Satan to torment me, to keep me from being too elated. Three times I appealed to the Lord about this, that it would leave me, but he said to me, 'My grace is sufficient for you, for power is made perfect in weakness.'

Her name was Elizabeth Walker. She asked me to go to her apartment in the retirement community to read one of her poems. Her mobility was limited, as she used a walking frame. It took us thirty minutes to make the short trip. I began to realize what it meant for an older person not to be able to move quickly. Yet she moved with such grace, and with a smile on her face. So many elder friends have taught me to view pain through the lens provided to them by a gospel that sees strength in weakness, power in powerlessness and life in death.

Paul had some real problem that plagued his life. He called it a 'thorn in the flesh', and whatever it was, he was stuck with it for life. Scholars have debated what this thorn was. Some have claimed it was epilepsy, others fading eyesight or malaria. Whatever it was, it hampered his work as a missionary. But

Paul received an answer to his prayer: 'My grace is sufficient for you, for power is made perfect in weakness.'

Older people are stuck with many thorns in the flesh. But the reality of the spiritual life may intensify as we struggle with our infirmities. In reality, old age may not be such a wonderful experience as often depicted by those who paint too golden a picture of old age. Even those who do not live in poverty, loneliness and neglect may find ageing a difficult time. In the rush to be too optimistic and supportive of older people, we may not take seriously the very real problems they experience as they grow older. Paul's pain was in not receiving healing from whatever infirmity had caused him distress, but he lived through it. He learned the great truth that God's grace is sufficient, and God's power is made perfect in weakness. So it still is for you and for me when we are stuck.

PRAYER

Help us, dear Lord, to be patient in tribulation and to accept gladly those weaknesses that will not go away. Help us to rely on your all-sufficient grace.

109

CARRYING BURDENS WITH OTHERS

Brothers, if someone is caught in a sin, you who are spiritual should restore him gently. But watch yourself, or you also may be tempted. Carry each others burdens, and in this way you will fulfill the law of Christ... Each one should test his own actions. Then he can take pride in himself, without comparing himself to somebody else, for each one should carry his own load.

Paul makes it clear that every person has to carry his own load and be responsible for his or her own life. No one can do that for the other person. This does not mean that we ignore others or become oblivious to their burdens. Paul says we cannot carry burdens *for* others, but we can carry burdens *with* them.

Caring for older people has special significance, for the elderly confront us with the illusion of 'final cure'. Everyone has the hope that life will be better and that anxieties and worries can be cured—but this is not always the case. Many older people live on the edge of an abyss, and every day is a challenge.

We may not cure, but we can care—care when lost dreams are real and the losses hurt; care when broken relationships cannot be healed, and limitations serve as reminders of finitude. Caring means to be present to those who suffer and to stay present when nothing can be done to change the situation.

One elderly woman told me that although she suffers from painful arthritis and other problems of old age, she still gets out and helps others. She said, 'I can get so absorbed in my painful hip and my lonely week that I miss the opportunity to console a recently widowed friend.' The fact is, we need reminding that caring for others, sharing their burdens, helps to take us out of the narrow world of our own suffering. We can lighten the burden of our years when we care for others.

A woman in her 40s told me why she was devoting time to doing chores for an elderly lady who had no family. 'Look,' she said, 'this could be me some day, living alone, trying to make ends meet with meagre funds. Something could happen to me, and I wouldn't be able to carry on my usual work. I help her because it gives me hope that someone like me will be around when it's my turn.'

PRAYER

Lord, open my heart to some elderly person in need. Help me to be present to their anxieties and needs, always realizing that I cannot take their burden, but I can carry it with them.

110

EPHESIANS 2:1–10 (NIV)

SAVED BY GRACE... AT ANY AGE

But because of his great love for us, God, who is rich in mercy, made us alive with Christ even when we were dead in transgressions—it is by grace you have been saved... For it is by grace you have been saved, through faith—and this not from yourselves, it is the gift of God—not by works, so that no one can boast.

Dr G. Campbell Morgan went to visit a member of Westminster Chapel in London. He was saddened to learn that she was to be evicted from her house because she couldn't pay the rent. That was on Saturday afternoon. On Sunday morning, Campbell Morgan told his congregation that he wanted enough money to pay the woman's rent. They gave it to him.

First thing on Monday morning, he went to the woman's house with the money. He could hardly wait to tell her the good news. He hammered on the door, but there was no answer. Again knocking repeatedly, and getting no answer, he left feeling dejected. Later in the day, Morgan learned that the woman had been home all the time. She had been afraid to answer the door for she thought it was the landlord who had come to collect the rent. All the time she cowered in fear, her minister stood at the door with the money she needed.

What a powerful story to illustrate the gospel! We owe God much rent. As Paul wrote, 'We were dead in transgressions.' But God does not demand that we pay for our sins, nor could we ever merit or earn being right with God by our own efforts or achievements. Our salvation begins in the pure, unmerited goodness of God. By grace are we saved, through faith. All we need do is open the door and receive this gift, the offer of God's grace and mercy in Christ.

An elderly woman was part of a crowd visiting Westminster Abbey. She was amazed at all the splendour and magnificence of the Abbey. But she turned to her guide and softly said, 'Has anyone been saved here recently?'

Regardless of age, salvation is by grace, and all our acts of goodness are a response to that grace, living out our gratitude to the God who has already appeared at the door of our hearts, offering this priceless gift.

REFLECTION

Therefore, dear Jesus, since I cannot pay you,
I do adore you and will ever praise you,
Think on your pity and your love unswerving,
Not my deserving.

JOHANN HERMANN (1585–1647), TRANS. ROBERT BRIDGES (1844–1930)

111

PHILIPPIANS 3:12–16

REMEMBER TO FORGET

Not that I have already obtained this or have already reached the goal; but I press on to make it my own, because Christ Jesus has made me his own. Beloved, I do not consider that I have made it my own; but this one thing I do: forgetting what lies behind...

As I moved through the hallways of a nursing home, a woman in a wheelchair reached out to touch me; I stopped, held her hand and smiled at her. She whispered softly, 'Remember to forget.' I had no idea what she meant, nor did she explain her words. Her words puzzled me, for older people have a fear of forgetting. They get irritated when they can't remember names or dates, or where they put their glasses, or how much medicine they took that day. Later, as I pondered her words, they began to make sense.

In his letter to the Philippians late in his life, the apostle Paul wrote, 'This one thing I do: forgetting what lies behind...' No doubt Paul had some bitter memories of his persecution of early Christians, and how he hurt the early Church. That must be left behind. No doubt Paul also meant that his past achievements in the Christian life must be left behind. There were conflicts he could remember—with the

Jewish Christians at Jerusalem, with Barnabas over John Mark, and with the Judaizers in the Galatian churches. They must be left behind.

An elderly person has much to forget—regrets amassed over the years, the career not chosen, the road not taken, broken relationships, the things that might have been. What benefit is there now in mulling over these memories, accusing others or even oneself?

Forgiveness of ourselves and others is the order of the day—every day of our later years.

Leonardo da Vinci, who painted the masterful *Last Supper* in Milan, had a friend who had wronged him. When he came to paint the face of Judas at the supper, he painted the face of his friend. However, when he tried to paint the face of Jesus, his hand seemed paralysed. Only when he erased the face of Judas could he paint the face of the Master. You cannot paint the face of Christ in your life when there is unresolved hostility towards someone.

Forgiveness allows us to remember the past in a way, unhook ourselves from strangleholds of old hurts, and move on with life. Remember to forget! That dear lady in the nursing home taught me a valuable life lesson.

MEDITATION
Remember to forget! What do we need to forget?

112

PHILIPPIANS 3:12–17

HOEING TO THE END OF THE ROW

But this one thing I do: forgetting what lies behind and straining forward to what lies ahead, I press on toward the goal for the prize of the heavenly call of God in Christ Jesus. Let those of us then who are mature be of the same mind.

The apostle Paul, writing near the end of his life, made it clear that the Christian is always moving on, never content with the past, always 'straining forward to what lies ahead'. Using a metaphor drawn from the foot race, Paul suggested the runner going flat out for the tape, with his eye always on he goal, with its prize in store. Paul must have been thinking of Christian perfection, attaining to 'the knowledge of the Son of God, to maturity, to the measure of the full stature of Christ' (Ephesians 4:13). Christians cannot think that once we have turned our lives over to Christ we can simply coast into the heavenly city.

A good example is John Wesley, an Anglican priest, who established Methodism in the 18th century. During his lifetime, Wesley preached 42,000 sermons. On average, he preached three sermons per day. Riding horseback, he averaged 4500 miles each year, often riding up to 60 or 70 miles a day. When he was 83, John Wesley wrote, 'I have lived this day fourscore years; and by the mercy of God, my eyes are not wasted dim. And what little strength of body or mind I had thirty years since, just the same I have now. God grant that I may never live to be useless!'[23] We might say that Wesley hoed to the end of the row—he finished the job.

They tell us that in the British Library in London one can see 75 drafts of Thomas Gray's 'Elegy Written on a Country Churchyard'. Gray didn't like it the first way he wrote it, nor the second or the third. He was not satisfied until he had rewritten it 75 times.

Being a Christian means that we are never satisfied with our past achievements, but rewrite the story of our faith as long as we live. It also means that as life moves into its second stage, we find greater meaning in who we are, not what we do.

REFLECTION
Christ of the upward way,
My guide divine,
Where You have set your feet
May I place mine
And march and move wherever You have trod,
Keeping face forward up the hill of God.

WALTER JOHN MATHAMS (1851–1931)

113

PHILIPPIANS 4:1–7

PAUL'S PRESCRIPTION FOR ANXIETY

Rejoice in the Lord always; again I will say, Rejoice. Let your gentleness be known to everyone. The Lord is near. Do not worry about anything, but in everything by prayer and supplication with thanksgiving let your requests be made known to God. And the peace of God, which surpasses all understanding, will guard your hearts and your minds in Christ Jesus.

Older people live in an age of anxiety where we have an overload of concerns that weigh on our minds and grate on our nerves. We worry about fading eyesight, loss of mobility and whether we have sufficient resources to provide a safety net for financial needs. We worry about our children and our health, and live in terror of the day when we will have to leave our homes. Loss of control over our lives is a major cause of anxiety for older people. Sometimes we even magnify simple concerns until they become major anxieties.

Paul counselled the Philippians, 'Don't worry about anything.' Paul did not advocate shirking responsibility or careful planning. All worry is not bad. What we need to avoid is needless anxiety that kills the spirit. What was Paul's prescription for anxiety? 'In everything by prayer and supplication with thanksgiving let your requests be made known to God.' The way to be anxious about nothing is to be prayerful about everything. Prayer helps us to practise positive imaging. So often, chronic worriers tend to be preoccupied much of their time with fearful, negative thoughts. We replay in our minds, like a videotape, projections of what can go wrong and how bad things might be. Prayer, practising the presence of God, helps us to erase those tapes and replace them with positive thoughts. Prayer helps us turn over the control of our lives to God.

Sitting in a Roman cell as he wrote these words, Paul no doubt must have watched the Roman guards. So he concluded with the promise that 'the peace of God... will keep [literally, garrison] your hearts and minds in Christ Jesus.'

Many older people love the old hymn, 'What a friend we have in Jesus'. Reflect on one line from that hymn, and then practise Paul's prescription for anxiety.

REFLECTION
O what peace we often forfeit,
O what needless pain we bear,
All because we do not carry
Everything to God in prayer.
JOSEPH MEDLICOTT SCRIVER (1819–86)

114

PAUL'S ETHICAL WILL

Finally, beloved, whatever is true, whatever is honourable, whatever is just, whatever is pure, whatever is pleasing, whatever is commendable, if there is any excellence and if there is anything worthy of praise, think about these things. Keep on doing the things you have learned and received and seen in me, and the God of peace will be with you.

We all know about the usual kind of wills (that distribute your material possessions), and living wills (that put you in charge of dying with dignity), but ethical wills are much less known. The idea comes from Jewish tradition which states that in addition to passing down possessions from generation to generation, we leave the next generation our values and beliefs. An ethical will reflects the voice of the heart. Many have common threads running through many of them—important values and beliefs, important spiritual values, hopes and blessings for future generations, life's lessons. Ethical wills take steps to ensure the continuation of these values to future generations.

Ethical wills are most often written as a separate document and shared with family members and community while the writer is still alive. Adult children usually ward off this subject with denials and are not willing to face the mortality of their parents.

Paul left his ethical will to the family of God at the church of Philippi, a faith community he dearly loved. The virtues he commended were those of Greek moral philosophy. Perhaps the Christians at Philippi, under stress of persecution, were tending to be blind to what was good in the pagan life around them. Paul used the good in those values as an ethical will. Consider the values—true (includes both speech and fact), honourable, pure, pleasing, commendable. Paul urged them to 'think about these things'. Then Paul turned from pagan values to his own teaching. 'Keep on doing the things that you have learned and received and heard and seen in me' (v. 9). His teaching and his personal example were the real legacy that he left for the Philippians. On a gravestone somewhere in the British Isles, these words were written in memory of a missionary who had devoted his life to Christ: 'This man had the kind of life only Jesus Christ could explain.' Above all else, that is the greatest legacy.

REFLECTION

If you were to write an ethical will for your family, what values and beliefs would you list? What would be some of the lessons of life you would like your grandchildren to know?

115

2 TIMOTHY 1:3–7

A GRANDMOTHER'S LEGACY

I am grateful to God—whom I worship with clear conscience, as my ancestors did—when I remember you constantly in my prayers night and day. Recalling your tears, I long to see you so that I may be filled with joy. I am reminded of your sincere faith, a faith that lived first in your grandmother Lois and your mother Eunice and now, I am sure, lives in you.

Paul was reminding Timothy that his sincere faith was a legacy that came from his grandmother, Lois. No doubt she had taught the young Timothy the stories of Jesus and made them live through her own devotion and faith. We wonder where Lois received her faith. However, she faithfully transmitted that faith to her daughter, Eunice, and to her grandson, Timothy. My grandfather, Dr G. Campbell Morgan, wrote:

There is a sense in which faith cannot be transmitted by parents to children. Every individual must exercise faith for himself or herself. But it is also true that it is very difficult for some children not to believe, because of what they have seen of the power of faith in their parents or grandparents. We cannot bequeath faith to our children, but we can make it much easier for them to believe by our own faith.[24]

I scarcely knew my grandfather who wrote these words, but his faith influenced me. We were separated by years, and the Atlantic Ocean, and I was with him on only two occasions when he was in the States. After entering the parish ministry in 1953, I began a lifelong study of his sermons and writing, and through those biblical expositions the faith of this prince of the pulpit was transmitted to me. Of course I had to work through my own issues for a personal faith, but my grand-father's books paved the way. They were his treasured legacy that he handed down to his grandson. Even how, almost 60 years since his death on VE Day in 1945, they remain his testimony of faith, a legacy I will leave for my own grandchildren.

We are blessed when we can receive the faith from parents and grandparents. But we must forge our own faith, and then leave that for future generations. Receive the faith… leave the faith. That is what grandmother Lois still teaches us.

PRAYER
Help us, loving Father, to appreciate the religious heritage we have been given, and then give us grace to hand that heritage down to future generations.

116

2 TIMOTHY 4:1–8 (NIV)

PAUL'S EPITAPH

For I am already being poured out like a drink offering, and the time has come for my departure. I have fought the good fight, I have finished the race, I have kept the faith.

I have spent a lot of my time in cemeteries and graveyards, leading more funerals than I can remember. I have memories of winter days with the casket sheltered by a tent, and cold, blustery winds causing the tent poles to clang in the wind, while families stand hushed and still as goodbyes are expressed. Walking among the graves, I have found words written on stone that tell us what the person wanted us to remember, or words that families wanted us to read.

Epitaphs fascinate me. Although the Bible occasionally refers to tombstones, no reference is made to words that might have been carved on them. The oldest known Christian epitaph pertains to Abercius, a second-century Phrygian bishop. At his request, this was his epitaph: 'I am the disciple of the pure shepherd'. On his tomb is the first use of the acrostic ICHTHUS, meaning 'Jesus Christ, Son of God, Saviour'.

The apostle Paul was writing to Timothy near the end of his

life. He talked about his death, that the time for his departure had come. The word used for 'departure' is a nautical term; it suggests a ship that has been moored to the shore, the rope flung off, the anchor lifted, and the ship moving out of the harbour into the wide and boundless sea. For Paul, death was casting off the ropes that bind us to this world and sailing into unknown waters, the life beyond.

Paul's epitaph summarized his life and ministry: 'I have fought the good fight, I have finished the race, I have kept the faith.' What higher testimony could there be for this ambassador for Christ? His mission to the Gentiles had been realized. Despite opposition and hardships, he had kept the faith. What a different epitaph was left to an earlier Saul, who late in his life said to David, 'Surely I have acted like a fool and have erred greatly' (1 Samuel 26:21, NIV).

Theologian John Shea says that 'whenever our biographies are deeply probed, a root metaphor appears which gives unity and meaning to our lives'.[25] How would you describe the root metaphor that gives unity and meaning to your life?

REFLECTION

Write three sentences as the epitaph or root metaphor of your life.

117

A REQUEST FROM AN OLD MAN

Therefore, although in Christ I could be bold and order you to do what you ought to do, yet I appeal to you on the basis of love. I then, as Paul—an old man and now also a prisoner of Christ Jesus—I appeal to you for my son Onesimus, who became my son while I was in chains. Formerly he was useless to you, but now he has become useful both to you and to me. I am sending him—who is my very heart—back to you.

How many times I have read Paul's short letter to Philemon, but only recently did I realize Paul's reference to old age. Philemon, a noble citizen of Colossae, had a servant Onesimus, who had robbed him and fled to Rome, where he met Paul, who was then a prisoner there for the first time. The apostle took compassion on him, received him with tenderness and converted him to the faith.

Paul, now an old man, sent Onesimus back to Philemon. He appealed to Philemon that he accept Onesimus as a Christian brother.

Onesimus means 'useful', and Paul played on the name by saying that Onesimus had become so useful to him that he didn't know what he would do without him. Paul hoped that

Philemon would receive the boy back, 'no longer as a slave, but... as a dear brother' (v. 16, NIV).

It's not known whether or not Philemon forgave Onesimus and let him return to be the old saint's comfort in prison. However, years later, when Paul was long since dead, another saint by the name of Ignatius was in jail. The bishop of Ephesus had sent some friends to visit him, and Ignatius wrote asking that some of them be allowed to stay. Ignatius in his letter used some of the same language that Paul had used in his letter to Philemon, as if Ignatius was trying to remind the bishop of something. The name of the bishop was Onesimus. Although there is no proof that this was the same slave-boy grown old, who became a bishop, it is tempting to think so. If so, useless had become more useful than Paul had ever dreamed.

In front of the Faculty of Medicine at the University of Madrid, there is a sculpture of a young man on horseback, ready to begin a race. He reaches back to receive a scroll extended by an old man. The old man's face is serene and full of integrity. That is what old man Paul did for Onesimus, the slave-boy. He extended to him the gospel of Christ that changed his life.

PRAYER

Lord Christ, as older people, help us to share the gospel with the younger generation, that they may run the race of life with faith and joy.

118

2 PETER 1:3–11

PREPARE NOW FOR AGEING

For this very reason, you must make every effort to support your faith with goodness, and goodness with knowledge, and knowledge with self-control, and self-control with endurance, and endurance with godliness, and godliness with mutual affection, and mutual affection with love. For if these things are yours and increasing among you, they keep you from being ineffective and unfruitful in the knowledge of our Lord Jesus Christ.

Abraham Joshua Heschel once wrote, 'People are anxious to save up financial means for old age; they should also be anxious to prepare a spiritual means for old age... Wisdom, maturity, tranquillity do not come when we retire.'[26] How true! We prepare for old age all our life. We bring to old age the person we create throughout life. People can be so absorbed in their work and family during their middle years that ageing takes them by surprise. They have not refined their lives with qualities that will still be there when they become old. Your final years will be a work of art if seen as part of a life begun not at retirement but at birth.

Sigmund Freud believed that subconsciously we remain the same age throughout our life. Whatever the physical changes, whatever the calendar says, there remains the constant person that I have been and will continue to be. So the time to prepare for ageing is not when we retire, but all through life.

The second letter of Peter makes a similar case for the Christian life. Christians are to make every effort to grow toward Christ-likeness. Being a Christian is a lifelong task. And all through life we are to grow in the faith. A ladder of virtues is mentioned, as Christians are to add these qualities one upon the other in an ascending scale, until love crowns the whole. Faith is the starting rung of the ladder, and love is the top rung. Some have compared these virtues with Paul's fruit of the Spirit in Galatians 5:22–23.

The second letter of Peter ends with a constant challenge for the Christian at any age: 'But grow in the grace and knowledge of our Lord and Saviour Jesus Christ' (3:18). A little girl fell asleep as soon as she sat down in church, and when her mother nudged her, she said, 'Sorry, I must have gone to sleep too near the place I got in.' That can become true of growing old or growing in the Christian life!

PRAYER

Father, help me now to prepare for old age by storing up qualities which make that last stage of life more than just living out the days.

119

1 JOHN 3:1–3

PLUS ULTRA

Beloved, we are God's children now; what we will be has not yet been revealed. What we do know is this: when he is revealed, we will be like him, for we will see him as he is. And all who have this hope in him purify themselves, just as he is pure.

The end of old age is death. We cannot be like the proverbial ostrich and bury our heads in the sands of daily life. Old age is the ante-room in which we wait for death. We may sit there for a short time or a long time, as we do in a doctor's waiting-room. But we can be sure that, sooner or later, death will open the door and call us. We can't be like the woman who told her husband, 'I don't care which one of us dies first, I'm moving to the coast.' Death is the final stage of life, and each of us resists dying with every fibre of our being; and it must be so, for death is life's most powerful enemy.

That is why the words of 1 John mean so much to older people: 'When he is revealed, we will be like him, for we will see him as he is.' This is our blessed hope, that God will grant us our resurrection bodies when death knocks at the door. We know very little about the next life. But we can be sure we will share Christ's resurrection.

Before Columbus set sail to cross the Atlantic, people believed that the world ended somewhere past Gibraltar. The Spanish royal motto said, *Ne Plus Ultra* ('There is no more beyond here'). But when Columbus returned, having discovered a new world, the suggestion was made to Queen Isabella that the motto should be changed by deleting one word. Now it read *Plus Ultra* ('More beyond').

The end of our earthly pilgrimage is not decline but arrival, and the door that opens at death leads to a fuller, more beautiful life. For the Christian, Christ's resurrection means that Good Friday or Holy Saturday is not the final word. The death and resurrection of Christ remind us that Easter will come.

In Bach's B minor Mass, at first we hear the mournful wailing of strings: '*Et sepulchrus est*' ('And he was buried'). There follows an awesome silence. The director raises his baton, and all the timpani and trumpets and all the singers burst forth with '*Et resurrexit!*'—'And he rose again'. There is more beyond!

PRAYER

God of the living, help us to believe that beyond death is life, and that as death could not hold Jesus, neither can it hold us.

120

1 JOHN 4:7–21

REPEATED REFRAIN OF AN OLD CHRISTIAN

Beloved, let us love one another, because love is from God; everyone who loves is born of God and knows God. Whoever does not love does not know God, for God is love.

He had been a powerful preacher in former years, but now old age had ravaged his body. He was feeble, crippled by arthritis, and nearly blind. 'No one asks me to preach any more,' he said, 'because they're afraid I will fall out of the pulpit. I have preached for fifty years, but I have only one message: God is love.'

This servant of God reminded me of the apostle John. Jerome reports a tradition that, at the very end, John had to be carried to the church in the arms of his disciples and used to say no more at their meetings than this: 'Little children, love one another.' At length, the disciples and fathers who were there, wearied with always hearing the same words, said, 'Master, why dost thou always say this?'

'It is the Lord's command,' was his reply, 'and if this alone be done, it is enough.'

God is love. Why is it that this understanding of God, found in this small corner of the Bible, seems to sum up all the rest? How does it come to be there and nowhere else; and how does that little sentence seem to epitomize our understanding of God? It is because we associate it so much with Jesus. John had been present in the upper room when Jesus spoke these words of the new commandment, 'I give you a new commandment, that you love one another. Just as I have loved you, you also should love one another. By this everyone will know that you are my disciples, if you have love for one another' (John 13:34–35). It was Jesus who placed love at the centre of the confession of God so unmistakably that John returned again and again to love as the central fact of the Christian life. It was his repeated refrain.

Several years ago, I heard of an unusual end-of-year address at a church training college. Instead of the usual words, the speaker said simply, 'Centuries ago Jesus of Nazareth said, "Love one another." I have nothing significant to add.' And neither do I.

PRAYER

God of love, help us to show love each day of our lives, for love remains the Christian's final word.

NOTES

1. Carl G. Jung, *Modern Man in Search of a Soul* (Harcourt, Brace and Co., 1933), p. 109.

2. G. Campbell Morgan, *Searchlights from the Word* (Oliphants, 1952), p. 16.

3. Henri J.M. Nouwen, *A Letter of Consolation* (Harper & Row, 1982), p. 16.

4. Richard Bach, Illusions: The Adventures of a Reluctant Messiah, Bantam, 1977, p. ii.

5. G. Campbell Morgan, 'Fifty Years—and After', *The Westminster Pulpit* (1913).

6. Ram Dass, *Still Here: Embracing Ageing, Changing, and Dying* (Riverhead Books, 2000), p. 204.

7. Quoted in Thomas Cole (ed.), *The Oxford Book of Aging* (Oxford University Press, 1994), p. 50.

8. Malcolm Cowley, *The View from 80* (The Viking Press, 1980), pp. 2–3.

9. Mary Pipher, *Another Country: Navigating the Emotional Terrain of our Elders* (Riverhead Books, 1999), p. 322.

10. Edwin Markham, 'Lincoln, the Man of the People', st. 4

11. Jean Vanier, *Community and Growth* (DLT, 1991), p. 140.

12. In Andrew J. Weaver, Harold G. Koenig and Phyllis C. Roe (eds.), *Reflections on Ageing and Spiritual Growth* (Abingdon Press, 1998), p. 49.

13. Campbell Morgan, *Searchlights from the Word*, p. 140.

14. Carol M. Bechtel, 'The Courage To Be', *Presbyterians Today*, November 1999.

15. F. Crossley Morgan, *A Psalm of an Old Shepherd* (Marshall, Morgan & Scott), p. 21.

16. Ronald Blythe, *The View in Winter* (Harcourt, Brace, Jovanovich, 1979), p. 5.

17. David Steele, 'Living with Mortality', *Presbyterian Outlook* (21 February 2001).

18. G. Campbell Morgan, *The Crises of the Christ* (Pickering & Inglis, 1945), p. 177.

19. John O'Donohue, *Anam Cara* (HarperCollins, 1998), p. 14.

20. William Barclay, *And He Had Compassion on Them* (The Church of Scotland Youth Committee, 1955), p. 130.

21. Vivian E. Greenberg, 'Therapy at 65: Becoming Wise' in *Aging and the Human Spirit* (Vol. 9 No. 1, Spring 1999), p. 4.

22. Henry Drummond, *The Greatest Thing in the World* (Greeting Books), p. 54.

23. Nehemiah Curnock (ed.), *The Journal of Rev John Wesley MA* (Epworth Press, 1960), p. 428.

24. Campbell Morgan, *Searchlights from the Word*, p. 357.

25. John Shea, *Stories of God: An Unauthorized Biography*, Thomas More Press, 1978, p. 56.

26. Abraham Joshua Heschel, *The Insecurity of Freedom* (Farrar, Straus, and Giroux, 1951), p. 79.

FURTHER READING

Ronald Blythe, *The View in Winter* (Harcourt, Brace, Jovanovich, 1979).

Thomas Cole (ed.), *The Oxford Book of Ageing* (Oxford University Press), 1994.

Malcolm Cowley, *The View from 80* (Viking, 1980) (out of print).

Ram Dass, *Still Here: Embracing Ageing, Changing, and Dying* (Penguin/ Putnam, 2000).

Miriam Dunson, *Very Present Help: Psalm Studies for Older Adults* (Geneva Press, 1999).

Rachel Z. Dulin, *A Crown of Glory: A Biblical View of Ageing* (Paulist Press, 1988) (out of print).

Kathleen Fischer, *Winter Grace: Spirituality for the Later Years* (Upper Room Books, 1995).

J.G. Harris, *Biblical Perspectives on Ageing* (Fortress Press, 1987) (out of print).

G. Campbell Morgan, *The Crises of the Christ* (Oliphants, 1952).

G. Campbell Morgan, *Searchlights from the Word* (Oliphants, 1952) (out of print).

Richard L. Morgan, *The Best Is Yet To Be: A Book of Readings for Older People* (BRF, 1999).

Mary Pipher, *Another Country: Navigating the Emotional Terrain of Our Elders* (Penguin/Putnam, 1999).

Stephen Sapp, *Full of Years: Ageing and the Elderly in the Bible and Today* (Cokesburg, 1987) (out of print).

BIBLICAL INDEX

ALSO BY RICHARD MORGAN

THE BEST IS YET TO BE
A BOOK OF READINGS FOR OLDER PEOPLE

The Best is Yet to Be celebrates both the challenges and the opportunities of the later years of life, with an easy-to-use 'daily readings' approach. Using a wide selection of Bible verses and quotations from a variety of authors and poets, the 62 meditations explore different experiences and themes common to this time of major life changes. How do we handle our memories? How can we learn to face our fears? What different values do we need to help us reach a place—or state—of peace and joy? Each meditation is accompanied by a suggested Scripture passage, a printed Bible verse, and a reading for reflection, plus a prayer.

ISBN 1 84101 075 8   £6.99
Available from your local Christian bookshop or, in case of difficulty, direct from BRF:
Tel: 01865 319700
Fax: 01865 319701
E-mail: enquiries@brf.org.uk
Website: www.brf.org.uk